D0513841

The GIRLS' BOOK of GLAMOUR

A GUIDE TO BEING A GODDESS

WRITTEN BY SALLY JEFFRIE
ILLUSTRATED BY NELLIE RYAN
EDITED BY LIZ SCOGGINS
DESIGNED BY ZOE QUAYLE

The GIRLS' BOOK of GLAMOUR

A GUIDE TO BEING A GODDESS

BUSTER BOOKS

For the lovely Kate Jeffrie

First published in Great Britain in 2008 by Buster Books,
an imprint of Michael O'Mara Books Limited,
9 Lion Yard, Tremadoc Road, London SW4 7NQ

www.busterbooks.co.uk

Text and illustrations copyright © Buster Books 2008
Cover design by Angie Allison (from an original design by www.blacksheep-uk.com)
Cover illustration: Paul Moran

All rights reserved. No part of this publication may be reproduced, stored in a retrieval
system, or transmitted by any means, without the prior permission in writing of the publisher,
nor be otherwise circulated in any form of binding or cover other than that in which it is
published and without a similar condition including this condition being imposed
on the subsequent purchaser.

A CIP catalogue record for this book is available from
the British Library.

ISBN: 978-1-906082-13-0

12 14 16 18 20 19 17 15 13 11

Printed and bound in November 2012 by Clays Limited, St Ives plc, Popson Street,
Bungay, Suffolk, NR35 1ED, UK.

Papers used by Michael O'Mara Books are natural, recyclable products
made from wood grown in sustainable forests. The manufacturing processes
conform to the environmental regulations of the country of origin.

CONTENTS

NOTE TO READERS

The publisher and author disclaim, as far as is legally permissible, all liability for accidents, injuries or loss that may occur as a result of information or instructions given in this book.

The most glamorous girls use their best common sense at all times. Be very careful with scissors, needles, kitchen equipment and hot liquids and get permission from the appropriate adult before using any tools or utensils. Stay within the law and local rules, and be considerate of other people.

HOW TO MAKE A GOOD FIRST IMPRESSION

First impressions usually last so follow these pointers to make everyone's first thoughts of you the best they can be.

• Remember to introduce yourself and ask the other person's name.

• Look them in the eye, smile and remember to speak clearly.

• Pay attention to what the other person is saying.

• Ask questions about their interests and hobbies.

• Just be yourself.

HOW TO TAKE A COMPLIMENT

There's nothing like receiving dozens of compliments to build up your confidence, even if you flush with embarrassment at first. It's a good idea to use these top tips for the next time a friend says something lovely about you.

• DO smile and say 'thank you'.

• DO be modest.

• DO compliment them in return.

• DON'T frown, mumble or look at the floor.

• DON'T just say 'I know'.

• DON'T disagree.

HOW TO DESCEND A STAIRCASE

A vital part of glamour is impressing people and there's no better way than with a grand entrance. Whether you're arriving at a ball or just trying to wow your friends at school, descending a staircase with style and grace can make a great impression. Here are some pointers for making the best entrance ever – and avoiding any embarrassing slips, trips or falls.

• Pause at the top of the stairs and gaze confidently around the room for a few seconds until everyone turns to look at you. This way you are sure to make maximum impact.

• Discreetly check the staircase ahead for any obvious hazards or obstacles before you take a step.

• If you are in a long ballgown, make sure you lift up the bottom of your dress so you don't tumble.

• Lift up your chin, smile and then lightly grip the handrail to help you keep your balance.

• Step gracefully out onto the first stair, keep smiling and remember not to look at your feet.

• Walk carefully and steadily down the stairs until you reach the bottom. *Voilà.*

HOW TO FLATTER A FRIEND

An essential part of glamour is making other people feel great about themselves, too. So don't just focus on yourself – add an aura of niceness to your personality. Remember to compliment your friends and classmates on their best qualities and you'll soon see how good it makes them feel about themselves.

THINGS YOU SHOULD SAY

- 'Your hair looks lovely.'

- 'I love your drawings.'

- 'You're really talented.'

- 'That really complements your eyes.'

- 'You've got really nice handwriting.'

- 'You're so well coordinated.'

- 'You're so good at sport.'

THINGS YOU SHOULDN'T SAY

- 'That's so last season.'

- 'Get with the programme!'

- 'You shouldn't wear that colour again.'

- 'What on Earth are you wearing?'

- 'Hahahahahaha.'

HOW TO CUSTOMISE YOUR SCHOOL UNIFORM WITHOUT YOUR TEACHER NOTICING

It is possible to express your own style even if you have to wear a school uniform. Here's how to do it without risking a detention.

• Find out about your school's uniform policy and check it thoroughly for any loopholes. How much you'll be able to customise your uniform depends on how strict your school is. Don't go too far and risk detention!

• Most schools don't insist you wear a particular size or length – within reason. For instance, if you like loose clothes then opt for a blazer in a slightly larger size so it hangs in a baggy style.

• If you have to wear a tie, think about how you'll wear it – perhaps you'd like it very short with a fat knot, or maybe you'd prefer it long with a thin knot. Experiment.

• Check out sales of second-hand school uniforms – most schools have them yearly. Designs of school uniforms subtly change over the years and you might prefer the vintage style of a second-hand item to the new ones currently in the shops.

• Investigate which items you're allowed to choose for yourself and then really express your taste with them. For instance, backpacks can be transformed with a clutch of decorative key rings, shoes can be updated by adding coloured laces and a new hairstyle can be created with different clips and grips.

• If your school only insists that you wear certain colours rather than specific items of clothing, you're really in luck. You'll be

able to experiment with a wide variety of great styles
while sticking to the colour rule.

• Get to know when your teachers are most likely to enforce
uniform rules. For instance, it may be fine to look a bit more
casual at break time so long as you smarten up for assembly.

• Remember – it's definitely your personality, not what
you wear, that really matters.

HOW TO EAT YOUR WAY TO BEAUTIFUL SKIN

Lotions and potions are great and smell lovely, but the very best way to get beautiful skin is from the inside out, which means eating a skin-friendly, healthy diet.

WATER WORKS

You should drink plenty of water throughout the day to keep your skin clear and bright. Aim for about six glasses a day to keep your levels topped up and avoid any fizzy drinks, which are full of sugar.

FRESH AND FRUITY

You should try to eat at least five portions of fresh fruit and vegetables every day. Skin-friendly superfoods include carrots, broccoli, apricots, strawberries, watercress and oranges. They're great for the rest of your body, too.

GREAT NEWS!

Experts can't find any evidence to link eating chocolate with having problem skin, so you can still indulge in the occasional choc-attack.

PERFECT DAILY MEAL PLAN

It's important not to skip meals – a regular, healthy diet can work wonders on your skin and give you lots of energy.

Breakfast. Start with a glass of fresh juice, wholegrain cereal with chopped banana and milk, followed by toast and honey.

Lunch. Make a cheese or ham sandwich on wholemeal bread with salad followed by yoghurt and fruit.

Dinner. Go for grilled chicken and a baked potato with fresh vegetables, followed by fresh fruit salad with yoghurt and nuts.

Snacks. Don't go hungry between meals. If you feel peckish try a healthy snack to keep you going. Fruit, nuts, vegetable sticks, crackers, yoghurt or a slice of wholemeal toast are far better for you than sweets or crisps.

HOW TO MAKE YOUR OWN LIP GLOSS

To give your lips a delicious glow you need a great lip gloss, but there's no need to spend a fortune – it's easy to make your own.

Gather together the following ingredients:

- 30 ml/2 tablespoons of petroleum jelly
- 5 ml/about 1 teaspoon runny honey
- 2 drops food flavouring – peppermint, strawberry or vanilla are particularly good
- A sprinkle of ultra-fine glitter from an art and craft shop (optional).

Mix all the ingredients together until thoroughly blended. Transfer the mixture to a small, clean pot or jar and apply regularly to your lips for a stunning shine.

HOW TO PUT ON A FASHION SHOW

This is a really glamorous way for you and your friends to fill a rainy afternoon. Get everyone to bring a selection of their favourite clothes, accessories and jewellery. Then take it in turns being the stylist, model and photographer at your own catwalk show.

You'll need:

• A camera.

• A great soundtrack you can strut your stuff to.

• Some adults to watch the final show (optional).

THE STYLIST'S JOB

• Select a stunning outfit for your model to wear.

• Chew gum and talk loudly on your mobile phone.

• Wear enormous sunglasses while you dress your model.

THE MODEL'S JOB

- Chew gum, talk on your mobile and demand things.

- Look bored while reading an important work of literature.

- Perfect your 'model walk' – head high, shoulders back, placing one foot directly in front of the other as though you're walking a tightrope.

- Most importantly, never smile.

THE PHOTOGRAPHER'S JOB

- Talk to the model as you take her photograph saying things like 'Love the camera, darling', 'That outfit looks divine' and 'Look this way, this way – wonderful!'

THE FINAL SHOW

Set up a 'catwalk' in the living room with chairs or cushions either side for your audience. Allow the audience in, get the music playing and send your model up the catwalk while the photographer takes shots of her and the audience applauds wildly.

HOW TO GET THE SHINIEST HAIR EVER

If your hair's looking dull and dirty, it's time to take some action. A few extra treats will soon have it back to its shiny, healthy best.

- **Be A Water Baby.** Just as drinking lots of water can help brighten your skin, a good dose of H_2O can keep your hair shiny, too.

- **Little And Often.** If your hair is looking less than glamorous lather up regularly with a mild shampoo to keep the dirt at bay.

- **Shampoo Dry Hair.** If your hair is ultra-dirty try applying the shampoo straight onto dry hair – leave for a couple of minutes before you get to work with water.

- **Get Conditioning.** Condition your hair regularly to guarantee silky, shiny tresses. This easy recipe works really well and saves you valuable cash.

You'll need:

- 5 ml/1 teaspoon of runny honey
- A dash of vinegar
- 50 ml/3 tablespoons evaporated milk.

Mix the ingredients together in a bowl and cover your hair from root to tip. Wind a warm towel around your head and wait for 20 minutes before rinsing thoroughly. The milk will cleanse your hair, while the honey nourishes and the vinegar adds a gloss. Yummy.

- **Rinse, Rinse, Rinse.** Rinse your hair under the shower until the water runs completely clear to be sure no shampoo or conditioner is left behind – it will just make your hair look dull and drab again.

• **Get Brushing.** Groom your hair once or twice a day to remove built-up dirt and dead skin cells. Always brush thoroughly before you wash your hair to allow the shampoo to move easily through it.

Top tip. There's no point brushing your shiny hair with a dirty brush. Wash your brushes and combs regularly in a bowl of warm water with a dollop of shampoo and leave them to dry on a towel.

HOW TO AIR KISS

Make sure you make a cool impression when you bump into friends. It's time to perfect the celebrity-style 'air kiss'.

Start by making sure that you look delighted to see your friend. Smile and widen your eyes and exclaim at how lovely she looks saying 'Darling', 'Honey' and 'Sweetheart' at the same time. Finally swoop towards her and almost touch her left cheek with yours and then her right cheek while saying 'Mwah' loudly each time.

HOW TO MAKE YOUR OWN BUBBLE BATH

Bubbles make a bath a special treat and you can save money by making your own.

Mix together 120 ml/½ cup of baby shampoo, 180 ml/¾ cup of water and a few pinches of salt. Finally, stir in a few drops of essential oil (lavender, lemon or peppermint are especially nice).

Pour the mixture into a pretty bottle. Try to find a plastic one, which won't break if you drop it. Decorate the bottle with stickers and a pretty ribbon and enjoy your bath!

HOW TO TURN BATHTIME INTO A RELAXING TREAT

This bubble-icious bath is best taken just before bed. Get all your chores and homework done first so you can R-E-L-A-X.

SET THE SCENE

- Make sure the bathroom is warm with clean towels ready.

- Have a cup of juice or water nearby, ready to sip as you soak.

- Put on some music and light a scented candle – a lavender one smells especially delicious and is very relaxing.

• Add a little scented bubble bath or oil to the running water – but take care not to leave the bath slippery for the next person.

Top tip. The heads of flowers floating on the surface of the water add a serious touch of glamour.

R-E-L-A-X

Sink into the water and lie there for 20 minutes. Rest your head on a bath cushion or a rolled-up towel and breathe slowly and deeply. Lie there and imagine all the worries of your day dissolving into the water.

AFTERWARDS

Pat your skin dry with a warm, soft towel. Smooth your skin with a little scented body lotion, taking special care of really dry areas like knees and elbows. Pull on your PJs and head straight for bed. Sprinkle a couple of drops of lavender oil on to your pillow to help you drop off.

HOW TO PERSUADE YOUR BEST FRIEND TO LEND YOU HER CLOTHES

A clever way to DOUBLE the size of your wardrobe is to share clothes with a friend. However, if your most stylish friend doesn't seem keen on letting you borrow her clothes, you need to learn how to use the art of persuasion...

- Compliment her on her brilliant taste in clothes and stress how much you'd love to be as well-dressed as her.

- Explain that you'd like to experiment with clothes more but you don't have enough money to buy lots of new things.

- Offer to let her take her pick of your wardrobe if she'll lend you something in return. (If you haven't got many clothes it may be best to wait until your friend has agreed to swap before you let her see the contents of your wardrobe.)

- Promise to wash and iron her clothes before you give them back to her. You will even dry-clean them, if necessary.

- Promise to give her clothes back on an agreed date – and stick to that date to ensure she's happy to swap with you again.

Top tip. Be very careful with your friend's clothes – if you ruin them she'll never let you borrow anything again.

HOW TO QUICKLY SMOOTH AWAY DRY HANDS

Keep a tube of hand lotion by your bedside at all times and remember to apply a drop every morning and evening to keep your skin soft and smooth. But, if your skin is still very dry, try this mini treat:

1. Run yourself a warm bath.

2. Cover your hands in oil – olive oil from the kitchen is fine, although manicurists prefer almond oil. Take the time to rub the oil into your nails, too, as it will help them to grow stronger.

3. Smooth on lots of rich hand lotion – it'll create a barrier around the oil and encourage it to sink into your skin.

4. Now soak in the bath for 10 minutes, allowing your hands to rest in the water.

5. When you get out of the bath, gently rub your hands dry, then apply a few more drops of hand lotion.

You'll be amazed at the results!

HOW TO APPLY
EYE-SHADOW

When you're ready to start experimenting with make-up it's a good idea to practise your technique at home before you unleash your new look on the world. Look for flattering, natural shades in a powder finish to highlight the colour of your eyes:

Blue eyes... pastel pinks or peach shades

Brown eyes... olive green or golden brown

Green eyes... lilac or gold

Hazel eyes... greys and mauve.

Make sure your parents are happy for you to try make-up and then start saving your pocket money for your favourite colours. Most make-up ranges offer eyeshadows in sets of three shades, which makes it even easier to find great colours to suit you.

Start with a little of the palest shade to highlight your brow line. Next brush the medium shade across your eyelid, avoiding the inner corner. Then use the darkest colour around the crease of your eye socket to define the shape of your eye. Blend the colours where they meet. Easy peasy.

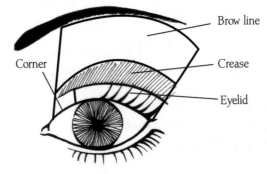

Brow line

Corner

Crease

Eyelid

HOW TO DEAL WITH ZITS

Even supermodels sometimes get spots. However, with a little know-how you can help a spot to heal quickly and make it almost invisible to the naked eye. Here's the low-down...

HOW TO CURE A SPOT

Firstly, you should NEVER squeeze a spot – it'll just look even more red and inflamed. What's more, you'll risk pushing the infection deeper into your skin and it may leave a permanent scar.

1. Wash your skin thoroughly and pat dry with a clean towel.

2. Wrap an ice cube in a clean hanky and hold it over the spot for a minute or two – it'll help bring down the swelling.

3. Dip the end of a cotton bud into some diluted tea tree oil (available from your chemist) and dot a tiny amount directly onto the spot.

4. Leave it alone to get better.

Top tip. If you keep getting spots in the same area, check they are not being triggered by contact with a telephone, cycle helmet or sunglasses, which aren't spotlessly clean. Check they are not caused by leaning on your hands.

HOW TO USE CONCEALER

Concealers are a great way to cover spots and blemishes so your skin looks perfect. You can buy them from the make-up counter at most chemists and department stores. Don't choose one that's darker or lighter than your natural skin-tone – you'll draw more attention to the problem.

1. If the spot's dry and crusty, apply a little petroleum jelly first to soften it.

2. Apply the concealer to the spot using a clean cotton bud. (Don't apply concealer on areas around the spot that don't need it or you'll just create a 'halo effect'.)

3. Pat some face powder over the concealer to set it and help it stay put all day long.

Top tip. Don't apply concealer with your fingers or you'll risk spreading infection.

IMPORTANT INFORMATION

If you feel you might be suffering from acne rather than just the occasional spot, make an appointment with your family doctor to ask for advice.

HOW TO MAKE YOUR OWN BODY GLITTER

This fabulous gel can be smoothed onto your body to make your skin shimmer. You can even smooth it through your hair for a gorgeous night-time glow.

What you'll need:

- 5 ml/1 teaspoon of petroleum jelly.
- 20 ml/4 teaspoons aloe vera gel. Aloe vera gel is used to soothe sunburnt or sore skin – it's easy to find in chemists and healthfood stores.

- Ultra-fine glitter (try art and craft stores).
- A small jar. Baby food jars or spice pots are ideal. Make sure they are thoroughly washed out in soapy water.
- A small bowl.
- A spoon.

How to make it:

1. Spoon the aloe vera gel into the bowl. Add the petroleum jelly to make it a little thicker. Stir well.

2. Sprinkle a few pinches of glitter into your mixture. Stir well.

3. Smooth a little onto the back of your hand to see if you like the effect.

4. If it's too glittery, add a little more aloe vera gel. If it's not glittery enough, add an extra pinch of glitter.

5. Keep going until you like the results.

6. Spoon the mixture into your jar.

7. Smooth on the glitter whenever you like and glow, glow, glow!

HOW TO HAIL A BLACK CAB SUCCESSFULLY

If you and your family have taken a trip to the city you may need to hail a cab to get home. Follow these top tips and impress everyone with your incredible cab-hailing skills.

1. Make sure that someone in the family has plenty of cash to pay for the journey.

2. Stand out. Wearing bright colours will help. Stand confidently near the edge of the pavement in a spot where you and your family are easy to see from the road.

3. Keep an eye on the road ahead for the next available taxi. Usually there will be a light on top of the car showing that the cab is not taken by another passenger.

4. As soon as you spot a cab raise your arm and wave elegantly to catch the driver's attention. Never step into the road as this is dangerous. Wait for the taxi to pull over to you.

5. Get into the cab and tell the driver your destination.

6. Sit back and relax. Perfect – your parents are impressed and you are nearly home.

(Make sure you only take a taxi when you are with your family and friends. It is safer that way and you have a ready-made audience to wow.)

HOW TO MAKE YOUR CLOTHES SMELL NICE

Never, ever mix up clean clothes and dirty ones. Put dirty clothes straight into a laundry bag or basket, ready for washing.

- Air your clothes at the end of each day by putting them on a clothes hanger or the back of a chair near an open window. Pop your shoes on the windowsill at the same time – it will help to prevent any unpleasant smells developing.

- Put scented tumble-dryer sheets into your shoes when you're not wearing them to keep them smelling fresh.

- Unwrap a bar of scented soap and place it in the bottom of your wardrobe as an instant clothes freshener.

- Add a few drops of perfume to the final rinse when washing your favourite woollies. They'll smell gorgeous when you snuggle into them.

HOW TO JAZZ UP A BORING PONYTAIL

A simple ponytail can be morphed into lots of new styles. With a little know-how and some practice you'll soon have the best ponytail around.

WRAP IT

Pull a strand of hair out of the ponytail. Wrap it around the top of your ponytail until the hair elastic is hidden. Secure in place with a hair clip.

KNOT IT

Separate your ponytail into six to eight strands. Twist each strand around and around until it forms a loose knot. Pin each knot randomly onto the back of your head.

CURL IT

Curl the ends of your ponytail with self-sticking rollers. Simply twist the rollers into slightly damp hair and leave them in until it's dry. When you remove the rollers, spritz the curls with hairspray to help them last for ages.

CRIMP IT

Pull a few random strands of hair loose from the ponytail. Crimp them with a heated crimping iron then let the tendrils fall around your face

PLAIT IT

Simply plait a ponytail and secure the end with a hair elastic or pretty hair bobble.

ACCESSORISE IT

Grab some pretty clips, hair snaps or other hair jewels and attach them all around the base of your ponytail. Alternatively, brush your hair into a low-slung ponytail at the nape of your neck. Tuck a few feathers – peacock feathers are fantastic – into the hair elastic.

DIP IT

Grab a sachet of temporary hair dye (the sort that washes out straight away – not permanent or semi-permanent). Follow the instructions on the packet carefully but only apply the dye to the ends of your hair. It should look as though your ponytail has been dipped in colour. Experiment with funky colours – black, red or orange are great with this look.

HOW TO HAVE A GOOD NIGHT'S SLEEP

A good night's sleep helps you feel great and look gorgeous. Most glamorous girls need around ten hours sleep each night. Try this mini bedtime routine to help you float off to the Land of Nod.

HAVE A LIGHT SNACK

Sweet treats, heavy meals and sugary drinks just before bed will keep you awake. If your tummy's rumbling, have some warm milk, a banana or a slice of wholemeal toast an hour before bed. A cup of peppermint or chamomile tea will help you relax, too.

WIND DOWN

Try to relax during the hour before bed by reading a book or listening to some gentle music. Make sure you get your homework done earlier in the evening – doing it just before bed will leave your mind racing and keep you awake.

ENSURE YOUR BEDROOM'S DARK AND QUIET

Make sure the curtains are pulled tight and ban any ticking clocks. If you live in a noisy household, make a 'Do Not Disturb' sign for your bedroom door and use it.

PREPARE FOR BED

Put a glass of water by your bed in case you wake up thirsty. Pull on some comfy PJs, wash your face, clean your teeth and hop between the sheets. Read for a while until you feel nice and sleepy then turn out the light.

GET COMFORTABLE

Make sure your neck is well-supported with one or two soft pillows. Don't wrap yourself up in too many blankets – you don't want to get too hot in the night.

LET YOUR WORRIES FLOAT AWAY

Worrying can keep you awake. If you're anxious about something, try this trick: Imagine you're putting the problem into a box. Then imagine you're putting the box into a cupboard and locking it away till morning. This often helps you relax enough to drop off.

Good night...

HOW TO BATHE LIKE CLEOPATRA

Cleopatra, the queen of Ancient Egypt, was said to bathe in milk. You too can take a milk bath to soothe and soften your skin.

Just add two pints of whole milk to a tub of warm water. Swirl it around thoroughly, so that the water goes white. Hop in and have a good soak for at least 20 minutes. Rinse in clear cool water.

HOW TO DO A PERFECT PIROUETTE

Find a good place to practise your pirouette. Carpets are not good at all so try the tiles in your kitchen or bathroom. Make sure there's enough space that if you fall you won't crash into something and hurt yourself.

Start with your left foot turned out and the heel of your right foot against the toes. This is called 'fifth position'.

Lift your right arm as though you are hugging a beach ball to your chest and hold your left arm out to the side, slightly curved towards your body.

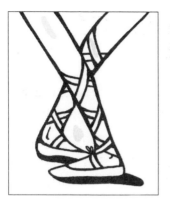

Then the difficult bit. Keep your back straight and in one movement bend your knees outwards in a *'plié'*, push up onto the tiptoes of your left foot and bring your right foot up to your knee with your toes pointed. At the same time use your momentum to spin clockwise.

When you have turned full circle, lower yourself off tiptoes onto your left foot and bring your right leg back into its original 'fifth position'. Always take the weight of your body on your supporting leg when you finish your pirouette.

Top tip. It's a good idea to learn how to 'spot' so that you don't get dizzy spinning around. Practise slowly at first to get the technique just right. Keep your eyes on one 'spot' on the wall. Slowly spin your body round, keeping your head in the same position until you can't turn anymore. Then whip your head around at the last possible second to the same spot again while you continue to turn. Perfect.

HOW TO MAKE
SOAP-ON-A-ROPE

Hanging the soap up in the shower means it's always easy to find – it makes a great gift, too.

You'll need:

- Three bars of white soap
- Cheese grater
- Bowl and jug
- Piece of rope, ribbon or garden twine
- Waxed or greaseproof paper
- Rubber gloves
- Food colouring.

1. Finely grate the soap into a large bowl.

2. Fill the jug with warm water. If you want to make coloured soap, add a few drops of your chosen food colouring to the water – don't over do it though, or you'll find your skin changing colour as you wash!

3. Add drops of the warm water slowly to the soap flakes until it's the consistency of thick porridge.

4. Pull on the rubber gloves and mix well with your hands.

5. Cut the rope, ribbon or twine into your chosen length (30–40 cm is ideal) and lay onto the waxed paper.

6. Pat the soap mixture around one end of the rope in a ball shape, making sure the rope is in the centre of the soap ball.

7. Once you're happy with the shape, leave the soap to dry for around 24 hours.

8. Tie a loop in the other end of the rope so that you can hang it up in the shower.

Top tip. You can add a handful of other ingredients to the soap mixture to ring the changes.

• Dried flowers look and smell very pretty.

• Porridge oats turn a simple soap into an effective body scrub.

• Grated lemon peel makes a refreshing soap that will really wake you up in the morning.

HOW TO GET THE FLUTTERIEST LASHES

A slick of mascara is the best way to create a fluttering fringe to your eyes – especially if you have light-coloured hair and your lashes are harder to notice. Here's what you need to know:

Most mascaras are applied with a spiral brush at the end of a wand as this makes them quick and easy to use. Some contain fibres to add extra thickness and length to your lashes. For a girl on the go, waterproof mascara is the best choice. It will withstand tears, showers and swimming. However, remember you'll need a special make-up remover to take it off as it clings to your lashes more than ordinary mascara.

1. Start by applying mascara to your upper lashes first. Brush them downwards to begin with, then brush the lashes upwards from underneath. Use a tiny zigzag movement from side to side to prevent the mascara turning to lumps on your lashes.

2. With the tip of the mascara wand brush your lower lashes, using a gentle side-to-side technique. You can keep your hand steady by resting your elbow on a firm surface. If you've got a shaky

hand, try holding the edge of a tissue under your eyelashes while applying mascara to prevent it smudging onto your skin.

3. Comb through your lashes with an eyelash comb to remove any small lumps of mascara. This will prevent your lashes from clumping together.

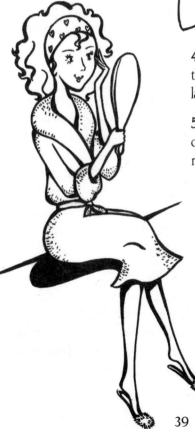

4. Take care not to blink while the mascara is still wet or your lashes will stick together.

5. Repeat the whole process once or twice more to create a really fluttery effect.

HOW TO WORK OUT YOUR FACE SHAPE

Different hairstyles suit different face shapes. The four main face shapes are oval, round, heart-shaped and square.

To work out what shape your face is, pull all your hair back from your face with a hairband. Look in a mirror and trace around the outline of your face with a lipstick (the sharp edge of a bar of soap will work well, too). Move away from the mirror and look carefully at the shape. Decide which shape your face is most similar to, then check out the description and choose from your ideal hairstyles. (Don't forget to clean the mirror afterwards!)

OVAL

Any style suits an oval face so you
can try really dramatic looks like
ultra-short bobs and 'urchin' crops
as well as long, straight hair.

ROUND

You would suit chin-length bobs, soft layers or side partings.

HEART-SHAPED

SQUARE

Try neat styles with flipped-up ends. Long wispy fringes, waves or short and spiky cuts would also work well for you.

Go for soft layers, curls, side-swept partings or hair swept onto your face.

HOW TO MAKE YOUR EYES LOOK BRIGHTER

If you're feeling tired and you've stared at a computer screen for too long or you're simply fighting off a cold, your eyes might start to look really red. Here's how to make them sparkle again with a simple three-step plan:

1. A lack of water can make your eyes look really tired so drink a litre and a half of water every day to banish redness.

2. Empty an ice cube tray into a sink of cold water and soak a flannel. Wring the cold flannel out, then lie down and place it over your eyes for five minutes. If the flannel gets too warm, soak it in the iced water again and repeat.

3. Apply a dot of pale, pearly eyeshadow on the skin at the inner corner of your eye and just above your pupil. This will make your eyes look wider and brighter even if you're still sleepy.

HOW TO PLAN A THEME PARTY

When it's time to celebrate it can be a great idea for you and your friends to throw a themed party. Get permission from the adults first then plan away.

• Choosing your theme might depend on the season, such as Halloween, Christmas or Summertime fun. Or you can just make one up – good ideas include Think Pink, Superheroes, Hawaiian or Hollywood. You could even base a party theme on your favourite TV show or on a particular era in history – Roman, Egyptian or the 1970s.

• Decide whether it will be a francy dress party or not. Your guests will need time to create their outfits to fit with your theme.

• Send out your invitations in good time and include all the information they need about the theme. Ask people to RSVP (this is French for *'Répondez S'il Vous Plaît'*, which means they need to reply) – this way you'll know how many guests to expect.

• The party decorations should go with your theme – for instance, hollow out pumpkins for Halloween, hang pink balloons and ribbons for a Think Pink party, drape furniture with white sheets and bunches of grapes for a Roman party.

• Keep your guests entertained with plenty of party games and dancing.

• It's a good idea to have music ready to keep the atmosphere lively. If you don't have lots of your own CDs you could ask your guests to bring along their favourites to dance to.

HOW TO MAKE A BAG CHARM

Glam up a plain handbag or a boring old schoolbag with a safety pin bag charm. It couldn't be easier.

What you'll need:

- 30 safety pins, various sizes
- Beads of various sizes
- Piece of thin elastic – about 15 cm

GET BEADING

1. Open up a safety pin. Thread as many beads as you can onto the pin – don't forget to get creative with the pattern.

2. Close the pin carefully.

3. Repeat this process for as many safety pins as you have.

4. Knot a bead on one end of the piece of elastic.

5. Now start threading the beaded safety pins onto the elastic. Thread some through the top end of the pin, some through the bottom end and some through the middle.

6. Finish off with two beads, secured with a knot.

7. Tie the remaining end of the elastic thread around the base of the handle of your bag.

HOW TO GIVE YOURSELF A MINI FACIAL

Every couple of weeks, set aside a bit of time to give yourself a relaxing salon-style facial at home. It'll help keep skin deep-down clean and super soft.

1. Smooth your skin with cleansing cream, gentle soap or facial wash. Leave on for one or two minutes to give it time to dissolve grime and make-up, then smooth away with a clean, damp flannel.

2. Massage a blob of facial scrub or some porridge oats over your skin to whisk away dead surface skin cells and clear blocked pores. Rinse away with warm water.

3. Fill a bowl with a kettleful of freshly boiled water (ask an adult to supervise this part). Then lean over the bowl, capturing the steam by placing a towel over your head. Stay there for five minutes to allow the steam to warm and soften your skin. Sensitive skins should skip this step.

4. Splash your face with warm water and pat dry.

5. Smooth on a home-made fruit face pack.

Oily skins. Crush six strawberries with a fork, smooth onto your face and leave for three minutes.

Normal/dry skins. Crush a peeled banana with a fork, smooth onto your face and leave for five minutes.

6. Remove the mask with a clean tissue then rinse your face with warm water.

7. Finish with a splash of cool water to freshen your skin. Pat dry with a towel.

8. Dot your skin with moisturiser and massage it in to encourage a brighter complexion.

HOW TO TELL A FRIEND SHE'S MADE A FASHION ERROR

Too shy to tell a friend her top is on inside out or her shirt is buttoned up wrongly? Don't be – she'll be less embarrassed if a good friend tells her straight away rather than letting her walk around looking really silly all day long. And you never know when you might need her to do the same favour for you!

Plan ahead. Get together with your friends and make up some subtle hand signals to warn each other – you could tug on your earlobe or sing a snippet from your favourite song. That way you'll know that you have each other's backs just in case the worst happens.

If you haven't prepared in advance for a fatal fashion disaster then the best thing to do is to quickly grab your friend and point out the error in your best quiet voice.

HANDY HINTS

• Compliment your friend on how well she handled the situation.

• Point out how great her taste in clothes is so who cares
if anyone laughed?

• Change the subject as soon as you can.

Top tip. Don't actually point. This will only draw attention to the
situation and embarrass her more.

THINGS TO AVOID

• Any kind of laughter – this will only draw attention
to the problem.

• Telling other people first – this is a quick way to end
a friendship.

• Doing an impression of how embarrassed she was.

HOW TO CUSTOMISE A T-SHIRT WITH FABRIC PAINTS

Wear your art on your sleeve as well as on the rest of your T-shirt by getting nifty with some fabric paints. The easiest way to create your own T-shirt design is with fabric pens – they allow you to paint directly onto the fabric without any mixing or mess and you can get them from most art and craft shops.

Here's how:

1. You'll need a plain T-shirt. Choose a plain white or pastel-coloured one so that your design shows up really well.

2. Practise your design on a piece of paper first. You could try graffiti-style, designing your own logo or just drawing a simple, bold image like a face or a sun.

3. Now you're ready to paint your T-shirt. Put a piece of thick paper or card inside the T-shirt so that the ink doesn't leak through from the front to the back.

4. Draw your image straight onto the T-shirt.

5. When you use fabric pens, you need to iron your finished design to help 'set' it. Check with an adult for advice or help before you do this.

Top tip. Once you've invested in a set of fabric pens, you can make use of them on lots of projects. Why not decorate shoe bags or pillowcases?

HOW TO CONVINCE PEOPLE YOU'RE A CELEBRITY

• Wear huge sunglasses that practically cover your whole face even when you're inside the house eating your tea.

• Go to school with a film crew (your kid brother and his friends will do). Explain to your teacher that you're the subject of a brand new reality TV show.

• Carry a huge handbag with a dog the size of a hamster in it.

• Apply fake tan from top to toe until you are bright orange.

• Wear very silly shoes.

• Be unreasonable wherever you go. You could tell the dinner ladies you're on a special diet and can only eat blue food or tell your teacher you didn't finish your homework because you were practising your Oscar acceptance speech.

• Get your parents to tint the windows of the family car.

• Travel with an entourage (a group of friends) at all times to help you with any boring tasks.

HOW TO TURN AN OLD PAIR OF JEANS INTO A FAB SKIRT

Here's the perfect way to recycle an old pair of jeans you don't like anymore into a skirt you'll love.

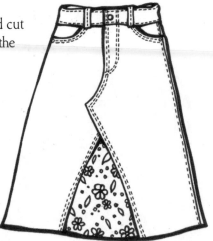

1. Take the pair of jeans and cut straight across both legs at the length you would like your skirt to be.

2. Cut carefully up the inside seam of each leg and trim off the extra fabric. At the front cut to just below the fly and overlap the curved sections. At the back cut to about 5 cm below the waist band.

3. On a flat surface overlap the curved sections at the front and back and sew into place.

4. From one of the pieces of cast-off legs, cut a triangle large enough to fill the gap between the legs (alternatively, you could use a pretty cotton fabric to contrast with the denim).

5. Either sew the triangles to the insides of the legs by hand or use a sewing machine.

6. Don't bother hemming the bottom of the skirt if you want to wear it straight away – the frayed look is very cool.

Top tip. If you're feeling creative sew a length of ribbon or lace trimming around the hem to add an extra touch of glamour.

HOW TO PERSUADE YOUR PARENTS TO LET YOU HAVE YOUR EARS PIERCED

If you really want to get your ears pierced you need to get permission first. It's worth planning in advance how to get your parents on your side. Whatever you do, don't let a friend pierce your ears for you – it's unhygenic and you'll risk an infection.

• Before you start on your campaign to convince your parents, be sure you really do want your ears pierced – there are some great clip-on earrings available that look just as good.

- Do your research first. The more knowledge you have, the easier it'll be to persuade your parents.

- Offer to pay for it yourself or suggest it would be a great birthday present.

- Visit a couple of ear-piercing shops with your parents first. They will be able to check who would do the procedure and the equipment that's used. Let your parents choose which place they prefer.

- Don't burst into tears or throw a tantrum if they refuse. Leave it for a while and ask again. Perhaps you'll eventually be able to persuade them to set a date when they'll allow you to have your ears pierced.

HOW TO LOOK AFTER NEWLY PIERCED EARS

Pierced ears might look good, but infected ears do not. Here's how to look after your newly pierced lobes properly:

- Make sure your first pair of earrings have gold posts (that's the part of the earring that goes through the hole). Gold posts are less likely to cause infection and swelling.

- When you first get your ears pierced, you should leave the earrings in for six weeks until your ears are completely healed. If you don't, your holes could close up and you'll have to go through everything all over again!

- Don't fiddle with your earrings during this healing process.

- Keep shampoo, soap and hairspray away from your ears.

• Apply antiseptic lotion to your ears morning and night – you should be given some by the person who pierced your ears. Wash your hands first, then apply the lotion to your ears with a clean cotton bud.

• Finally, rotate each earring once every morning and night.

WHAT IF YOUR EARS GET INFECTED?

An infected ear lobe may be swollen, red, warm and painful or oozing fluid. If you think one of your pierced ears may be infected, tell an adult immediately. They'll probably want to check with your family doctor for advice on how to deal with the infection. Follow any advice carefully to ensure your pierced ears become healthy again.

HOW TO SHAMPOO AND CONDITION YOUR HAIR PROPERLY

Scientists have worked out exactly how you should wash and condition your hair. After experimenting on hundreds of people, they came up with the following instructions:

SHAMPOOING

• Dampen your hair with running water warmed to a temperature of precisely 36.7 C°.

• Use exactly the right amount of shampoo – 6 ml of shampoo for short hair, 8 ml for medium length hair and 10 ml for long hair.

• Lather hair for 28 seconds, rubbing it 20 times with your fingertips.

- Rinse your hair for 22 seconds in water that's 36.7 C°.

- Repeat the whole process.

CONDITIONING

- Use 2 ml conditioner for short hair, 4 ml for medium hair and 6 ml for long hair.

- Apply conditioner with a wide-toothed comb.

- Leave the conditioner to sink in for 57 seconds before rinsing with water at 36.7 C°.

- Pat your hair dry with a towel to absorb excess water before leaving it to dry naturally.

You have been told!

HOW TO GET SUPER-SOFT FEET WHILE YOU SLEEP

DID YOU KNOW?

• There are 26 bones in each of your feet.

• Each time your feet hit the floor, double the weight of your body impacts with the floor.

• Over 50% of people don't like their feet, often as a result of foot problems.

• Your feet contain around 250,000 sweat glands and they perspire more than any other part of your body. Each foot produces an egg-cup-full of sweat each day.

• In your lifetime, it's estimated that your feet will carry you 110,000 km or almost three times around the world.

Indulge your feet with the following treat once a week and they'll always be soft and smooth...

1. Rub your feet with a layer of rich foot lotion. If you prefer, you can make your own by mixing 60 ml/¼ cup olive oil, 60 ml/¼ cup single cream and 20 ml/1 tbsp mayonnaise.

2. Pull on a pair of socks and head for bed.

3. Wash off the cream in the morning to reveal beautifully soft tootsies.

4. Don't forget to put the socks in the wash!

HOW TO GROW YOUR NAILS SUCCESSFULLY

If you regularly nibble your nails it's a hard habit to break but well worth trying if you'd like to grow elegantly long and strong nails.

Restrict yourself to biting the nails on just one hand and then on only one nail. You'll soon be inspired to grow out the bitten one.

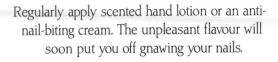

Regularly apply scented hand lotion or an anti-nail-biting cream. The unpleasant flavour will soon put you off gnawing your nails.

If your parents and school allow it, try using stick-on nails for a few weeks so your nails have a chance to grow underneath.

HEALTHY NAILS

Once you've broken a nail-biting habit follow these pointers to grow the perfect set of pinky tips. The secret to growing your nails is to make sure they are as strong as possible so...

• Eat two portions of protein a day. Meat, fish, dairy, soya and lentils will all help your nails to grow strong and healthy.

• When you wash the dishes make sure you always wear washing-up gloves – soaking your hands in water weakens the nails.

• When your nails begin to grow keep them in shape with a nail file or an emery board to prevent them breaking.

• Make sure your nails are dry, then gently smooth away any rough edges and file them into a nice, even shape.

• Never file down into the sides of your nails – it can lead to infection and seriously weakens your nails.

• Don't use your nails as a tool. Find the right tool for the job rather than risk having to grow your nail from scratch again.

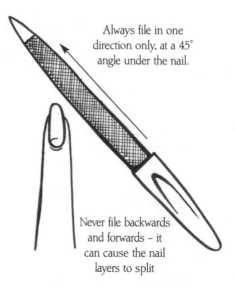

Always file in one direction only, at a 45° angle under the nail.

Never file backwards and forwards – it can cause the nail layers to split

• Once a week, soak your bare nails in a bowl of olive oil for 10 minutes. Then wipe away the excess oil with some cotton wool.

DID YOU KNOW?

• Nails grow about 3 mm a month.

• They grow faster in summer than in winter.

• If you've lost a nail due to an accident, it'll take about six months to grow back.

• Your middle finger grows the quickest while your thumbnail grows the slowest.

• A child's nail grows more quickly than an adult's.

• Toenails grow more slowly than fingernails.

HOW TO CONVINCE PEOPLE YOU'RE A HAND MODEL

Just having beautiful hands isn't enough – you have to act the part properly as well. Following these tips will help convince your friends that your hands are your fortune and provide you with a ready-made excuse for avoiding all sorts of boring tasks.

• Refuse to do anything that might damage your hands. This can include doing the washing-up (dries out the skin), writing essays (you could get ink on your fingers) and taking the dog for a walk (the dog's lead could cause calluses to form on your hands).

• Gather together a handful of props like a lipstick, a cup of coffee and a box of washing powder. Get your best friend to take close-up pictures of your hands holding the props – just like in the adverts. Mount the results in a photograph album and, *voilà*: your very own portfolio to show people.

• Wear white cotton manicure gloves to protect your hands at all times.

• Practise hand-modelling poses whenever anyone's around. Don't just pass your mum a magazine she wants to read – strike a 'hand pose' as you do it.

• Take up music lessons. Playing a musical instrument helps to encourage steady hands – vital for photographic shoots, which can go on for hours.

• Insist that you have jelly for pudding after every meal. Hand models say the gelatine in it is good for strengthening nails.

• Change the colour of your nail polish each night – after all, you need a new look for every single photo shoot.

• Get your parents to insure your hands for a million pounds.

HOW TO SHAPE YOUR NAILS TO SUIT YOUR HANDS

When you're filing your nails, make sure you bear in mind your overall hand-shape and pick a file-style that might suit you best.

• If you have small hands – go for almond-shaped nails.

• If you have quite short, wide fingers – aim for 'squoval'-shaped nails (which is just an oval with a squared-off tip).

• If you have large hands or wide nails try squared-off ends.

HOW TO BE THE BEST BRIDESMAID

It's a real honour to be asked to be someone's bridesmaid or flower girl. Here's how to impress the bride on her Big Day.

Smile sweetly when you see your dress for the first time. It doesn't matter if you hate lime-green satin – it's the bride's choice. Just comment on how clever of her it was to match your dress to her bouquet.

Have something to eat and drink before you put on your outfit. That way you won't spoil it with crumbs and you'll have energy to get through the day. It might be a long time before you get a chance to eat again.

Offer to look after younger bridesmaids or flower girls if there are any. Very young children have a habit of playing hide and seek under the bride's dress and bursting into tears during the ceremony.

If the bride has a long skirt and veil, make sure it's all straight before she enters the church or registry office. If you're the oldest bridesmaid, you'll need to take the bride's bouquet during the marriage service, then hand it back to her afterwards.

Offer to help out with small chores during the day such as getting the bride a drink of water while she's getting ready or handing out wedding cake to guests later on.

Most of all, smile and enjoy yourself.

HOW TO WALK WITH CONFIDENCE

The best way to make people think you're brimming with self-assurance and poise is to strut like a star. Follow these steps to get the best out of your stride.

1. Imagine that someone is pulling your head up with a long piece of string, push your shoulders back and smile.

2. Think of a fast-paced, lively song that you love and sing the tune in your head, or out loud if you prefer.

3. Gently start swinging your arms and walk along to the rhythm of your song, bouncing a little at the knees.

4. Heads will turn – just remember to smile and wave.

HOW TO CRY AT A WEDDING

There's nothing like a happy occasion to bring out smiles and tears. Here's how to get your fill of crying without upstaging the bride.

• Take a pretty cotton hanky with you rather than an old tissue – use it to dab gently at your eyes if you start to well up.

• Remember to smile and breathe while you are crying, you don't want to pull scary faces at a wedding.

• It's important not to sob too loudly or blow your nose noisily. This may prevent everyone else from enjoying the ceremony.

• Don't cry for too long or people will start to worry about you rather than thinking how beautiful the bride is.

HOW TO GET RID OF PUFFY EYES

If you've got a cold, hay fever or you're just really tired, try this de-puffing trick.

Stand a clean teaspoon in a glass of iced water. After a few minutes, remove it and hold the spoon against your closed eyes until they feel cooler and brighter.

HOW TO PRETEND YOU'VE GOT FRECKLES

If you have freckles, never try to hide them – they make you look naturally pretty and sun-kissed. If you're not lucky enough to have freckles, there's an easy way to fake them.

1. Start by making sure that your skin is really clean.

2. Choose a light brown eyebrow pencil if you have pale skin and a deeper shade if you have darker skin.

3. Sharpen the eyebrow pencil and dot a few freckles onto your face, concentrating them around your nose and cheeks.

4. To make your fake freckles look more realistic, apply different sized dots and soften the edges with a clean cotton bud.

5. Dust your skin with a little face powder to set them in place.

Top tip. For a speedy way to create an impression just draw on a 'beauty spot'. Take a black eyebrow pencil, and apply a firm dot to your skin about 2 cm from your top lip, then set it with a little face powder.

HOW TO EXIT A LIMO GRACEFULLY

Once you're a celebrity you'll be invited everywhere – and a stretch limousine is definitely the best way to arrive. But when all your fans and photographers are waiting to see you it's important to learn how to get out of the car without falling over yourself.

1. Open the door on the pavement side and check there's room for you to get out easily. Don't let camera flashes distract you.

2. While staying seated swing both feet out onto the pavement. Use the door handle and the frame of the car to gently push yourself up in one smooth movement. Do not rush this stage.

3. Remember to tilt your head forward a little to avoid banging it on the door frame as you stand up straight.

4. Shake out your dress to make sure you haven't wrinkled it then turn towards your waiting fans to smile, wave and head for the red carpet zone.

5. Pause for a moment or two for the waiting photographers and film crews. Don't forget to strike a pose (see page 118).

6. Remember to stop and give a few quick autographs to some of your fans before heading in to your glamorous event.

HOW TO MAKE A RIBBON BELT

Jazz up your tired old jeans with a pretty plaited belt made from lengths of colourful ribbon. Here's how to do it:

1. Look for ribbon that's about 2–3 cm wide.

2. Choose three different colours that all look good together.

3. Measure around your waist. Multiply this measurement by three – that's the length you should cut your ribbons to.

4. Take a strand of each colour. Tie them together in a knot at one end. Lay them on a table and start plaiting. You can plait it loosely or tightly – it's up to you!

5. Tie a knot at the end of the plait.

6. Form two more plaits from the remaining ribbons.

7. Now plait the three plaits together to make a fat ribbon belt. Secure each end with a knot.

8. Simply thread the belt through the loops of your jeans and show off your new style. Tie the two ends together to secure.

Top tip. To create a more glamorous effect just cut the ribbon strands a little longer and leave the ends loose to flutter around. You could even add a selection of pretty, glittery beads for some extra sparkle.

HOW TO CLEAN YOUR MAKE-UP BRUSHES

Make-up brushes are the best way to apply make-up but they can get dirty. Wash them every week or two to keep your brushes clean and your face healthy.

1. Squirt a little shampoo into a cup and top up with warm water.

2. Swish the brushes in the water to dissolve dirt and grime.

3. Rinse the hairs under a running tap until the water runs clear.

4. Gently squeeze the brushes with your fingers to remove excess moisture.

5. Place a clean towel on a flat surface and lay the brushes on top.

6. Leave them to air-dry.

HOW TO MAKE YOUR BEDROOM SKIN-FRIENDLY

Central heating can draw the moisture out of your skin, leaving it dry and dull, but there's a simple way to prevent this happening.

Keep the air moist in your bedroom simply by placing a well-watered houseplant on your windowsill or by keeping a bowl of water near a radiator. This way the water will gradually evaporate and humidify the air, keeping your skin moist.

HOW TO GET THE HAIR YOU REALLY WANT

If you're growing out your hair it can be difficult to avoid a few bad-hair days until you get the style you want. Have a regular trim to snip away split ends and keep your hair looking healthy. Tell your hairdresser what style you're aiming for – they will be able to trim your hair to help you reach your goal as quickly as possible.

It's easy to end up with a haircut you don't like unless you tell your stylist exactly what you want – follow these tips to avoid a really terrible hair day.

• Don't be shy about showing the hairdresser a photograph of the hairstyle you'd like. Be prepared for them to explain that the style might not suit your hair type or face shape – try to find a good compromise.

• Always use your fingers to show the stylist how long you want your hair, how much you want cut off and the shape you're after.

- Don't bury your nose in a magazine while your hair is being cut. Watch what the stylist is doing and politely but firmly stop them if they're about to make a mistake.

- Take a good look in the mirror when they have finished. It's your last chance to point out any problems and give your stylist the opportunity to put things right.

Remember – a good diet, regular exercise and plenty of sleep will encourage your hair to grow more quickly. Experiment with different looks as your hair goes through different lengths and invest in hair clips and hair elastics to add extra style as it grows.

HOW TO GROW OUT YOUR FRINGE

- Start wearing your fringe away from your face straightaway – use clips or a hairband to keep loose tendrils out of your eyes.

- Switch to a side parting so that your fringe still looks stylish as it grows out.

- Consider having some face-framing layers cut into the rest of your hair to help balance out your fringe as it's growing.

HOW TO CREATE YOUR PERSONAL STYLE

Following fashion slavishly can cost a small fortune. Be creative and thrifty and come up with a brilliant style of your very own.

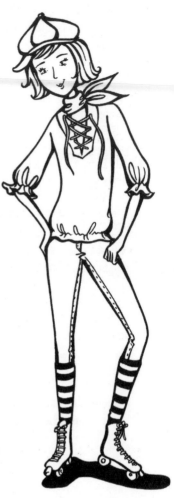

- Look for inspiration in magazines and on TV, then select the things you like most.

- Pick and choose the things you like and imagine how you could combine them into a style of your own.

- Lay all your clothes out in your room and sort them into piles of things that suit you and things you'd like to adapt.

- Try changing the length or adding extra trimming to items that are old and dull.

- Experiment with unusual combinations and try layering or adding accessories.

- Scour second-hand shops for fabulous bargains that suit your style and pick them up cheaply. It's the greenest way to shop because you'll be recycling clothes.

HOW TO ACCESSORISE BRILLIANTLY

You'll be surprised how many accessories you already have lying around at home. Anything from scarves and belts to brooches and bracelets can be used to add instant pizzazz to your wardrobe. Most of these ideas can be achieved with items you already own so you needn't spend any extra money.

• Tie the ends of a long scarf together and hook your left arm into the loop, then bring the scarf across your back and hook your right arm into the other end to make an instant shrug.

• If last year's coat is looking a bit bedraggled jazz it up with a pretty brooch or a fabric flower. Pin it on to a lapel or somewhere just below your collar bone.

• If your hair is misbehaving why not just cover it up? Take a scarf or a pretty top and wrap it around your head like a turban or a bandana. For extra sparkle pin on a glamorous brooch just above your forehead.

• When a cold winter breeze is getting to you simply fold your scarf in half, loop it around your neck and slip the ends through the loop. This will cut out all the draughts and look super-stylish.

• Gather together all of the bangles and bracelets you own and put them all on at once – they'll be very eye-catching and make a great noise at the same time.

• A pretty silk or chiffon scarf can be used for lots of different things – knot it at the neck, tie it at the waist or loop it around your wrist and tie it in a stylish bow.

HOW TO STOP CHLORINE IN SWIMMING POOLS DAMAGING YOUR HAIR

Swimming is a fantastic way to get fit, but it can wreak havoc with your poor hair. That's because the water in most swimming pools contains a chemical called chlorine which kills germs in the water and makes it safe to swim in. The trouble with chlorine, though, is that it can make your hair dull, dry and unmanageable.

• Coat your hair with some conditioner, then pull on a swimming cap to protect it against the chlorine in the pool.

• If you're too vain to wear a swimming cap, make sure you wet your hair under the shower before you get into the water. That way your hair will already be soaked and as a result will absorb much less of the chlorinated water.

• Shampoo your hair as soon as you get out of the pool using a special swimmer's shampoo – this contains ingredients to remove the chlorine from your hair.

• Use loads of conditioner after swimming to guard against the drying effects of chlorine on your hair.

Top tip. Chlorine can actually make blonde hair look a little green. If you have blonde hair and find this happens to you ask an adult to dissolve four soluble aspirin for you in a jug of water. Pour it over your hair and leave for five minutes, before rinsing. The juice of a lemon or a little vinegar in 500 ml/2 cups of water works pretty well, too.

HOW TO HAVE THE PRETTIEST SUMMER FEET

- Get three pretty shades of polish that go well together (pastels work best).

- Apply one coat of the first polish all over your toenails. Allow it to dry.

- Grab the second shade and paint a dot of colour in the centre of each nail.

- Take the last colour and place several dots around the centre, like the petals of a flower.

- Allow the polish to dry.

- Show off your new look by slipping on a pair of pretty flip-flops.

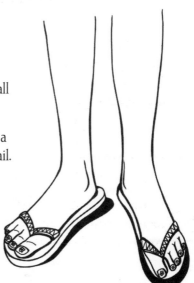

HOW TO HOST A SPA-STYLE PARTY

Impress and pamper your friends by inviting them round for a relaxing and luxurious beauty evening at your place. Ask everyone to bring a dressing gown, flip-flops, hairbands, a mirror and a face cloth.

Get the mood right by covering seats and tables with white sheets. Use lamps or, better still, fairy lights to create a relaxing atmosphere and switch on some calming music. Check out your local library for special CDs that are designed for relaxation (forest or ocean sounds are particularly mellow) for when you're having a foot massage – there are lots around.

Prepare some healthy spa-style snacks and drinks. Sparkling water or fruit juices look good in pretty glasses with colourful straws. Make special ice cubes to add to the drinks the day before. Pop slices of strawberry, lemon or lime into each section of an ice cube tray, then add water and freeze. A selection of fruit, popcorn and little sandwiches are good choices for mini-bites.

Top tip. Snacks on cocktail sticks are a great idea – your guests will find them easier to pick up if they have wet nail polish.

SPA TREATMENTS

Gather together a group of parents or friends to act as spa staff. Get them to set up separate 'beauty stations' offering different treatments. Create a poster board to outline which treatments are available, and let your guests pick the three they would like.

Nifty Nails. File away rough edges from nails with an emery board. Slick on clear nail polish, then sprinkle over some glitter while the polish is still wet. Seal in with a second coat of polish.

Sensational Stripes. Get a tube of 'hair mascara' or some brightly coloured eyelash mascara. Comb it through dry hair for instant, washable highlights. This looks great if you concentrate the colour in the front sections of your guest's hair.

Magical Masks. For each mask, mix together a teaspoon of runny honey, three tablespoons of natural yoghurt and a few drops of lemon juice. Apply to clean skin and pop cucumber slices over the eyes. Relax for five minutes and rinse.

Fruity Feet. Add a few drops of fruit-scented bubble bath to a large bowl of warm water. Get your guest to soak their feet for five minutes. Pat their feet dry then give them a foot massage using a few drops of olive oil or body lotion.

Glamorous Lashes. Start by curling your friend's eyelashes with a metal eyelash curler. Gently does it – take care not to pinch her skin or pull on the lashes. Then slick on a coat of clear mascara to add extra definition.

Top tip. Before your guests leave take a photo of each of them to show the quality of your salon. Pour everyone a cup of bedtime herbal tea so they're sure to enjoy a good night's sleep when they get home.

HOW TO CREATE YOUR OWN DRESSING TABLE

Create a little oasis of calm in your bedroom by organising all of your beauty goodies really nicely. Any table, shelf or windowsill will do – you could even set everything up on a tray covered with a piece of pretty fabric. Whatever you choose, the same rules apply.

• Too many things on display will look cluttered and gather dust. Keep your favourite items on show and store everything else in a selection of pretty boxes or bags – decorated margarine tubs and pencil cases are ideal.

• A cutlery tray makes it easy for you to organise all your stuff into sections – hair clips in one section, nail polish in another.

You can store it in a drawer or slide it under your bed and just bring it out whenever you need it.

• Try to get a good-sized mirror – it can be hand-held, free-standing or attached to a wall. You'll never look your best if you're constantly peering into a tiny compact-sized mirror.

• Make sure your dressing table is close to a good light source so that you can see what you're doing properly.

• Decorate your dressing table with a few pretty ornaments. Why not arrange shells from the seaside, a few wild flowers in a jam jar, or some cute trinkets from a charity shop?

HOW TO BEAT THE BLUES

Try one of these simple ideas to cheer yourself up the next time you're feeling a little down.

• Phone your best friend for a cheerful chat. Don't moan. Plan a great day out or weekend treat instead.

• Watch your favourite funny movie.

• Keep a memory box full of 'happy things'. A good rummage through old birthday cards, invitations and favourite photographs will clear the clouds.

• Put on your favourite music and dance away the blues.

• Pick some pretty flowers or interesting leaves and arrange them in a vase.

HOW TO CHOOSE THE PERFECT GLOVES

With so many options available it's difficult to know which glove to choose. Use this handy guide to help you select just the right one for any occasion.

• Long gloves, worn above the elbow, are perfect for a ball or other glamorous event but they will make it much more difficult to eat so make sure you have a snack before you go.

• Pink rubber gloves are essential for the washing-up to keep your hands looking gorgeous.

• At a wedding white lace is traditional, but can become itchy, so try to get satin instead whenever possible to prevent irritation.

• In winter, woollen gloves are best, but if you are somewhere particularly cold sheepskin mittens are ideal to help avoid chapped hands.

• If you're meeting the Queen opt for short silk gloves in case she wants to shake your hand.

HOW TO GET RID OF TANGLES

If your hair's really tangled up you'll need to take special care when you try to untangle the knots or you'll risk badly damaging your crowning glory.

1. Start by smoothing lots of conditioner over your hair – use olive oil if you haven't got conditioner.

2. Try to separate the strands using your fingers. Start at the ends of the hair and work up towards the roots. Keep going until you get most of the large knots out. Hold the hair near the scalp with one hand and use the other to untangle. That way, when you brush, there will be less pulling (and less pain).

3. Take a wide-toothed comb and work it gently through your hair from the bottom upwards. Rub conditioner over the teeth of the comb to help it glide through the hair really easily.

4. Finally, comb through the hair with a fine-toothed comb until all the tangles are removed.

5. Rinse out the conditioner once your hair is knot-free. Then shampoo and condition again.

Top tip. Do you wake up every morning with tangled hair? Try placing a rectangular silk scarf over your pillow while you sleep – it'll stop your hair fuzzing into knots.

HOW TO FRENCH PLAIT YOUR HAIR

This is a single braid that follows the curve of your head from the crown to the nape of your neck. A French plait is similar to a basic three-strand plait, except that you pick up extra strands of hair as you work your way down. As long as your hair is below chin-length you should be able to manage it. Get together with a friend and practise on each other.

Here's how to do it...

1. Separate the hair from ear to ear, across the top of your friend's head. Gather the top section and divide it into three equal strands as though you're making an ordinary plait.

2. Start by crossing the right strand over the centre strand, then bring the left strand across, just as you would with a normal plait.

3. Before you plait the third strand scoop up an extra section of hair taken from the loose hair directly underneath.

4. Carry on plaiting, but from now on, add an extra section of hair to each strand as you go. Try to take a similar amount of hair each time to keep the plait even.

5. The plait will naturally follow the curve of her head as you pick up and include the new hair. Keep going until you reach the nape of the neck and all of the hair has been included.

6. Finish by plaiting the rest of the hair to the ends and secure it with a pretty hair elastic or a ribbon.

HOW TO GET RID OF FLAKY LIPS

Cold weather or nervous nibbling can lead to sore, dry lips. Here's a great way to make them better again.

• Slick your lips with petroleum jelly.

• Leave it on for ten minutes to soften any hard flakes of skin.

• Cover your index finger with a damp flannel and gently massage your lips. This will remove the petroleum jelly and the bits of dead skin at the same time.

• Rub a little petroleum jelly or lip salve into your lips to prevent the problem happening again.

HOW TO HAVE THE BEST MANNERS

Make the most of good manners with these helpful hints.

- No matter how hungry you are it's still rather rude to push into the queue for lunch. As a general rule there should be plenty of food to go around, so there's no rush.

- Losing can be a strain so try not to sulk if you don't win every time. It can be just as hard not to be a gloating winner, too, so remember to congratulate everyone else for playing well rather than laughing at the losers.

- Although it's tempting to jump straight onto the bus or train when seats are scarce, other travellers will always appreciate it if you let them get out first.

- If you're trying to win an argument you're much more likely to get positive results with cool reason rather than a hot temper. If you start to feel steam coming out of your ears try leaving your persuasion campaign until you've calmed down a little.

- If a friend or relative is nice enough to give you a present it's a good idea to have a polite response ready just in case you're not sure what it is. Say things like 'Oh, I love it!', 'I couldn't have thought of something so original' and 'That'll be really useful'. Say 'Thank you' straight away, especially if you need to call or write. If you forget you might not be so lucky next year!

If you can manage all of that you are definitely a glamorous goddess!

HOW TO ORDER FOOD IN A RESTAURANT

If your family is going out for a special meal remember these top tips and you'll be able to order your food with style and ease.

• Don't be afraid to ask what something is if you are unsure – it's much better than getting a nasty surprise on your plate.

• Some restaurants have hundreds of items on the menu so don't bother to read the whole thing. Pick a section you like the look of and choose something from there.

• It's perfectly alright to order a drink first if you need more time to decide. Don't be rushed into ordering too soon.

• Take a peek at what people are eating at other tables. If they look as though they're enjoying their meal choose the same dish.

• Try not to order too much. There's nothing worse than over-indulging and feeling terrible afterwards.

• Be prepared to try something new – you might enjoy it.

Bon appetit!

HOW TO HAVE A WHITER SMILE

Sparkling teeth and fresh breath are a real beauty boost. These tips will help give you a head-start.

• Brush your teeth twice a day to remove plaque. This is the sticky layer that builds up on teeth and it is the main cause of tooth decay.

• Brush for at least two minutes each time. Hum along to some music while you do it to help pass the time more quickly.

• Don't forget to brush your tongue as well as your teeth. This will clear the surface of old food and help prevent bad breath.

• An old toothbrush can't do its job properly, so change yours every three months, or sooner if the bristles are splayed.

• Use dental floss regularly to clean between your teeth where your toothbrush just can't reach.

• Visit your dentist twice a year to make sure your teeth are in perfect health.

• A natural remedy for sweeter-smelling breath is to chew parsley leaves. They're rich in a chemical called 'chlorophyll' – Mother Nature's own deodorant.

• To help prevent tooth decay save sweets and sugary food and drink for an occasional treat.

• Keep your breath fresh by rinsing thoroughly with a mouthwash. You can make your own using a strong peppermint tea. Pour hot water over two tea bags and wait for it to cool before popping the cup in the fridge to chill.

• If you'd like really sparkling teeth you can even make your own whitening toothpaste. Baking soda has been used for years as a natural tooth whitener. It's really cheap and available in most supermarkets. Dip a dampened toothbrush into the soda, then gently brush your teeth to remove any stains and improve whiteness.

HOW TO LOOK BEAUTIFUL FOR FREE

The best three beauty treats of all are actually free – sleep, fresh air and lots of water.

• Breathing in fresh air literally oxygenates your skin so that it looks rosy and fresh.

• Most of us simply don't drink enough water. Two thirds of our bodies are made up of water.

• As well as boosting your energy levels, sleep gives your body the chance to repair and renew itself so you look even more beautiful the next morning.

HOW TO MAKE YOUR OWN JEWELLERY BOX

If you have lots of pretty bracelets, beads and rings you need somewhere special to keep them. It's easy to turn an old carton or container into your own decorated jewellery box.

What you'll need:

- An empty cardboard box – an old chocolate box is ideal.
- Various patterned papers to decorate with. Be as imaginative as you can. You could use pictures from old magazines and newspapers, old wrapping paper, used postage stamps, old musical scores or glittery stickers.
- Liquid PVA craft glue – the sort that dries clear.
- Fabric to line the box – anything from fun fur to velvet
- Scissors.

What to do:

1. Cut up your pieces of paper.

2. Glue the pieces of paper to the outside of the box, making sure they overlap. Keep going until the whole box is covered. If you want your box to look old, now's the time to 'age' the paper. While the glue is drying simply leave a tea bag in water for a few minutes, then brush the tea over the surface of the box and leave it to dry.

3. Brush a layer of glue all over the surface of the box. This helps protect the box and makes it look shinier.

4. Once the glue's dry on the outside it's time to decorate the inside. Simply cut your chosen fabric to fit inside the base, sides and lid of your box and glue into place.

5. When it's dry, fill your new jewellery box with all your favourite trinkets.

HOW TO REMOVE INK STAINS FROM YOUR FINGERS

Oh no! You have an important birthday party to attend but your pen has leaked all over your hands. Inky fingers are okay for school but not so good for parties, but it's easy to bleach away the stains with an ordinary lemon. Just cut the lemon in half and rub the cut side over the ink stains. Wash your hands in gentle soap afterwards, then rub in some hand cream.

HOW TO LOOK (AND FEEL) PERKY WHEN YOU'RE FEELING TIRED

When you've got a busy day ahead but you wake up feeling exhausted, here's how to perk yourself up.

• Freshen up with a tingly lemon shower gel. If you can bear it, switch the water on to cold just before you finish showering for an ultra-invigorating start to your day.

• Wash your hair while you're in the shower. Take the time to massage your scalp with your fingertips. It's a great pick-me-up.

• Eat some breakfast – it really is the most important meal of the day and gives you the energy you need to get going. Try wholemeal toast and a glass of orange juice, or a bowl of unsweetened muesli with a chopped banana and yoghurt.

• Try this simple deep-breathing exercise to increase your energy levels. Lie on your back, supporting your head with a cushion, and place your hands on your tummy. Shut your eyes and concentrate on expanding your tummy as you breathe in, and flattening it as you breathe out. Continue for five minutes.

• Your body needs lots of fresh air and daylight, so take a brisk ten minute walk at some point in the day and drink plenty of water to refresh you.

• Put on the spritz with a fresh-smelling body spray. It will lift your spirits and make you smell great, too.

• Gently pinch your cheeks to give them a red glow that will make your look instantly healthier.

• Lie down and place a cold tea bag over each eye for five minutes.
  There is an ingredient called 'tannin' in tea, which reduces
  puffiness in your eyes and makes them look brighter.

HOW TO GIVE YOURSELF A FACE MASSAGE

Just like every part of your body, your face will look better after a mini massage.

- Pour a few drops of olive oil into your hands and smooth it onto your face and neck.

- Use your fingers to stroke upwards from the base of your neck to your chin.

- Now stroke up one side of your face, then the other.

- Go around your nose and up towards your forehead.

- Stroke across your forehead from left to right, using one hand.

- Finish off by gently 'drawing' a circle around each eye using one finger.

HOW TO DO A FRENCH MANICURE

When it comes to nail trends, there's one look that never goes out of fashion and that's the French manicure. It leaves your nails looking clean, fresh and healthy, and it matches any outfit.

Here's how to do it:

1. The classic French manicure uses two coats of pale pink polish. Look for a natural shade without any extra sparkly bits.

2. The best way to apply nail polish is in three strokes – one down the centre of the nail and one stroke either side. Apply two coats, giving each one plenty of time to dry.

Top tip. To turn a French manicure into an 'American manicure', use a beige polish instead of a pink one.

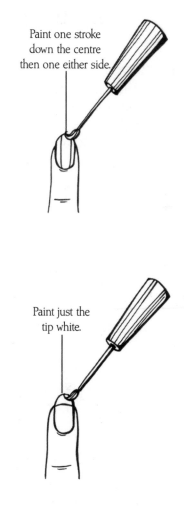

Paint one stroke down the centre then one either side.

3. Now it's time to paint the tips of your nails with a white polish. Be careful not to overload the brush or the varnish will flow down the bristles too quickly for you to control.

Top tip. Rest your hand on a firm surface to keep your hands steady and create a perfect finish.

Paint just the tip white.

4. Once the white tips of your nails are dry, paint on a clear topcoat of polish to seal in the colour and create a chip-free finish.

Top tip. If you're feeling impatient you can dry nail polish more quickly by blasting your nails with a cold jet of air from your hairdryer.

HOW TO LOOK YOUR BEST IN A PHOTOGRAPH

Make the most of any opportunity you get in front of a camera. Practise these useful pointers to make sure you always look your best.

- Brush your hair quickly in case it's sticking up and check that you don't have anything stuck between your teeth.

- Don't stand straight on to the camera, turn your body slightly to one side, but keep your head facing forward for a more natural pose.

- Don't look directly into the lens, look slightly to the side instead – this will help to you avoid 'red eye'.

- Press your tongue to the roof of your mouth, lift your chin slightly as though you are stretching to look over a high garden fence and smile. This way you'll avoid any unflattering shadows under your chin.

- If your photographer is using a flash widen your eyes a little just before the picture is taken so that you're not caught with your eyes closed.

- Try not to stand with your back to a light. You will only appear in silhouette, which will defeat the object!

- People always look good in a photograph when they are laughing – try to think of something funny just before the shot and you'll be caught at your best possible moment.

HOW TO MAKE AN ACCEPTANCE SPEECH

You've finally been nominated for an award and, suddenly out of all the nominees, the host announces that you're the winner! You have a limited time to make a dazzling acceptance speech so make sure yours is the one that people are talking about the next day. Follow these pointers to make the most of your moment at the mic.

• If possible choose a fun way to get onto the stage – run across the seats, cartwheel, crowd-surf or dance – anything, as long as you make a lasting impression.

• Remember to mention that it's an honour to be singled-out from such a wonderful group of nominees.

• Tears are fine, but make sure everyone can still hear you.

• Memorise a short list of the most important people to thank and then say 'Everyone else – you know who you are'.

• When the music starts playing, leave the stage immediately.

Top tip. If you don't win, remember to plaster a delighted-looking smile on your face and applaud loudly till everyone stops looking.

HOW TO MAKE WELLINGTON BOOTS WORK FOR YOU

Wellington boots might seem like a fashion no-no but with a little creativity and panache you'll be able to carry off a long walk through muddy fields easily. These tips are guaranteed to help you stay stylish in the country or the city.

• Look out for all the trendy wellie designs from funky flowers to colourful rainbows – even celebrities are wearing them to brighten up their winter outfits.

• Alternatively you could funk up your old wellies by using water-proof pens or acrylic paints.

• Always try to match your outfit to your boots. If you can coordinate with extra accessories, even better.

Now even on the dullest day you'll be able to stay stylish and make the most boring wellies a fashion must-have.

HOW TO GIVE A GREAT INTERVIEW

If you're about to give an interview to a magazine or TV journalist, it's important to prepare in advance. Good tactics can make a big difference and help you to leave a great lasting impression.

• When you meet the interviewer order a long, cool drink, such as a smoothie, to stop your throat getting dry. It will also come in handy if you are asked any difficult questions – take a long sip of your drink while you come up with a good answer.

• Don't forget to look the interviewer straight in the eye when you meet them. Shake their hand firmly and smile confidently – that way they'll know how friendly and open you are.

• Name-dropping can be impressive. Mention your favourite celebrities by their first names to convince the interviewer that you're the best of friends.

• If you're about to appear in your school play or sing in a talent contest bring it up as often as you dare – the more publicity you can get, the better.

• People will soon get bored of hearing about you if you give hundreds of interviews. Only pick your favourite magazine or TV show to talk to and give them an 'exclusive' instead.

• Make sure everyone knows how to spell your name correctly.

HOW TO MAKE YOUR OWN SIGNATURE PERFUME

This is the simplest recipe ever for making perfume at home. Just use your favourite garden flowers and herbs.

What you'll need:

• 240 ml/1 cup of water
• 1 cup of fresh flower petals, chopped
• Muslin square (or, failing that, a clean cotton dishcloth)
• Bowl and saucepan
• Pretty bottle.

What to do:

1. Spread the muslin in the bowl, letting the edges hang over the rim.

2. Fill with the flower petals and cover them with water.

3. Cover with a plate and leave to stand overnight.

4. The next day, carefully lift the muslin cloth out of the bowl and squeeze the scented water into a saucepan.

5. Get an adult to help you gently heat the scented water until only about an egg-cup-full remains.

6. Leave to cool, then pour into your pretty bottle.

7. Dab on your perfume and smell gorgeous. (Kept in the fridge, this perfume should last up to a month.)

HOW TO BLOW-DRY YOUR HAIR PERFECTLY

Keep your hair looking sleek and shiny with a salon-style blow-dry at home. This step-by-step guide will help you get it right.

1. Comb your hair gently after shampooing and conditioning to remove any knots.

(See page 79 if your hair's in a real pickle.)

2. Gently squeeze your hair to remove excess water.

3. Wrap your hair up in a towel for five minutes.

4. Get to work with your hairdryer. Make sure you blow-dry down the length of the hair from the roots to the tips – this makes the outer 'cuticle' of each hair lie flat, which means shinier hair.

5. Work the hairdryer quickly over your head, ruffling your hair with your fingers at the same time.

6. Tip your head upside down while you direct the dryer's nozzle at the roots – this will build body into your hair.

7. Only when your hair is just beginning to feel dry, start using a brush to style it – before that, you're wasting your time.

8. Style the front of your hair first – it's the bit that everyone will notice. Work your way around to the sides and back. It may be helpful to use clips to section off parts of the hair you're not working on.

9. Give your hair a final blast of cool air to fix the style.

10. Ruffle with your fingers – to add a little texture.

HOW TO SMELL GORGEOUS

Nothing says glamour like smelling great. Try out these tactics and you'll always be the sweetest-smelling girl around.

FRESH AS A DAISY

It goes without saying, but you should have a bath or shower every single day.

HERBAL REMEDY

Add sprigs of herbs to your bath for a natural treat. Refreshing ones to try are mint, rosemary and thyme – either raid the kitchen cupboard for dried ones or check out the garden for fresh herbs. Once the tub is full, toss in the herbs and let them float in the water to release their scent.

FULL STEAM AHEAD

Adding a few drops of perfume to the floor of the shower will create beautifully scented steam.

A FRESH START

Sprinkle a dry towel with your favourite fresh fragrance. Put it in the tumble dryer for a few minutes until it heats up and give yourself a vigorous rubdown. The hot fragranced towel will make you feel fabulously awake and alert.

SWEET DREAMS

Sprinkle your bedsheets with talcum powder! You'll wake up smelling lovely.

EAT THAI

Smell sweet with Thai food. Believe it or not, this type of food is said to produce the nicest body smells, so take the opportunity to eat lots of it! It contains plenty of aromatic ingredients, such as mint, lemon grass and coconut. Go easy on the garlic, though!

LAYERS OF LOVELINESS

Learn to layer fragrance to smell beautiful all day. Start with a scented bath oil, and soap. Move on to the body lotion and finish with *eau de toilette*. Put a perfume gift set on your next birthday or Christmas wish-list.

HOW TO TIE-DYE A T-SHIRT

The best way to brighten up a boring old white T-shirt is by tie-dyeing it. It's much easier than it looks to create a groovy sunburst design and add some hippy chic to your wardrobe.

What you'll need:

- A pack of cold-water dye in any colour you fancy
- Salt and a metal spoon
- Elastic bands to create the designs
- Rubber gloves to stop the dye staining your hands
- One measuring jug filled with cold water
- One washing-up bowl filled with warm water
- One white T-shirt (obviously!).

Top tip. Check that it's okay to use things from the kitchen before you start, or buy your own set specially for dyeing.

Here's how:

1. Prepare the mixture – open the dye container and pour the powder into the jug of cold water. Let it dissolve.

2. Add the bag of fixative and the required amount of salt. (Every brand of dye is slightly different, so read the instructions carefully.) Stir until everything's dissolved.

3. Pour the dye mixture into the bowl of warm water. Stir again until thoroughly mixed.

4. To prepare the T-shirt, pinch the fabric in the middle of the front. Securely twist an elastic band around the pinch. The sections of fabric covered by the elastic bands won't absorb the dye and will remain white.

5. Next, bunch the fabric together and tie a second elastic band around the pinch about 5 cm from the first.

6. Continue adding elastic bands, 5 cm apart, until the front of the T-shirt is completely wrapped.

7. If you like, repeat the same process again on the back of the T-shirt and even on the sleeves of the T-shirt.

8. Immerse your T-shirt in the bowl of dye. Push it down into the liquid with the spoon to make sure it's thoroughly wet.

9. Leave your T-shirt to soak for an hour then squeeze out the water and rinse away any excess dye.

10. Hang the T-shirt up on a line to dry, then remove the elastic bands. *Voilà*, a beautiful sunburst T-shirt.

HOW TO SOOTHE TIRED FEET

It's no surprise that at the end of a hard day at school (or at the shops) your feet can feel tired and sore. Try this quick and simple remedy to bring them back to life.

Start by soaking your feet in a bowl of warm water to which you've added a handful of sea salt. Keep them there for five minutes. Next, try lying down on your back on the floor with your feet up, resting on the edge of the sofa. Stay there for ten minutes.

HOW TO MAKE A DOOR CURTAIN

Create a glamorous entrance to your bedroom with a beaded door curtain. It looks fab and is easy to make.

What You'll Need:

- Thick piece of ribbon cut to the same width as your doorframe.
- About 30 plastic straws – any colour.
- 12 pieces of fishing line or strong clear thread, each 1.8 m long.
- Plastic beads – around 200.
- A few drawing pins to secure the curtain to your doorframe.
- Scissors.

How To Make It:

1. Lay the thick piece of ribbon on the floor. Secure each strand of fishing line to the ribbon at equal intervals – do this by looping one end of the thread over the ribbon and tying a knot.

2. Cut the straws into 5 cm lengths.

3. String the beads and straw pieces onto each length of fishing line, alternating them and finishing with a bead.

4. When the fishing line is full, feed the end of the thread through the bead twice – finish with a knot to secure in place.

5. Repeat for each piece of fishing line.

6. Get an adult to tack the curtain over your door with drawing pins.

HOW TO LIP-SYNCH SUCCESSFULLY

If you haven't got a good singing voice but want to become a pop star it's important to learn how to lip-synch. This is a kind of miming where you look as if you're singing a song even when you're not. Here are some tips to help you.

• Choose a simple song that you can really put your heart and soul into. Look for one that is funny, or very emotional, or which has a strong beat.

• Learn the lyrics! There's nothing worse than forgetting the words mid-performance.

• Really think about what the words of the song mean and aim to express this with your body language during your show.

• Don't be afraid to exaggerate your facial movements during your performance – the audience will really enjoy it.

• Dress up – it will really boost your confidence.

• Never turn your back on your audience – it will make it more difficult to keep their attention.

• Don't worry if you think people suspect you're lip-synching – some of the most famous singers do it. Concentrate on performing it as well as you can.

• If you're not confident enough to perform alone, get a friend or a group of friends to join you. There are plenty of duets and songs by bands to choose from.

HOW TO BE THE COOLEST PARTY GUEST

Follow these simple rules to take the party world by storm.

• Always be fashionably late – twenty minutes or so is ideal. After all, this party is just one of many on your social calendar. (Don't be too late though, you don't want to appear rude.)

• Smile and look around at everyone when you enter a room – even if you don't know anyone it will make people want to come and talk to you.

• Mingle with as many people as possible. Next time people will notice if you're not there and you'll probably end up with even more party invitations.

• Don't be the last to leave – even the best party girl has to get enough beauty sleep!

HOW TO MAKE A BUTTON AND BEAD CHARM BRACELET

What you'll need:

• A selection of pretty buttons. (Ask an adult if you can raid their sewing box for some, snip them off old, unwanted clothes, or scour charity shops and sewing stores for bargains.)

• A selection of pretty beads.

• Some elastic thread.

• Sewing thread, cut into 10 cm lengths.

What to do:

1. Measure enough elastic to fit around your wrist and then add on 8 cm extra. Knot the ends together and snip away any excess.

2. Take one bead or button at a time, and feed a length of sewing thread through its hole. Then secure on the thread with a knot.

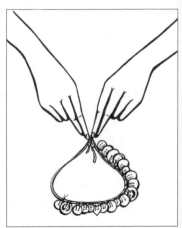

3. Now tie the button or bead around the elastic. Secure with a double knot and snip off the excess thread.

4. Keep on adding buttons and beads until you can't see the elastic any more.

Top tip. Cram as many buttons and beads onto the elastic as you can. The more they overlap, the better the bracelet will look.

HOW TO LOOK INSTANTLY TALLER

Good posture is the best way to add inches to your height. It'll make you look more confident, too. Look in a mirror and check yourself out.

- DO keep your neck straight from hairline to shoulders.

- DON'T let your head hang forward.

- DO keep your chest high and your shoulder blades flat.

- DON'T hunch up your shoulders or slump forward.

- DO stand tall with a shallow curve in the small of your back.

- DON'T stick your tummy out.

- DO tuck your bottom in.

- DON'T stand with your feet turned out – keep them parallel with each other.

HOW TO WRITE YOUR FIRST AUTOBIOGRAPHY

An autobiography is a real-life story, which you write all about yourself and your life. It is a great way to tell fans how you became famous, so it is a good idea to start making notes now.

- Keep a journal. When you look back you'll be able to remember exactly how you were feeling each day and use it to add lots of emotional touches to your story.

- Read the autobiography of someone you admire for inspiration.

- Ask your family and friends for any funny anecdotes they can remember about your early years. These are especially good if they show how talented you were, even as a baby.

- Remember to be totally honest. It's almost certain that someone will know if you have exaggerated anything, which could lead to embarrassment later on.

- Aim to have your first autobiography completed by the age of 16. That way you'll still have plenty of time to write the second and third volumes.

HOW TO PRETEND YOU CAN DANCE FLAMENCO

Fool people that you can dance the flamenco with this mini-routine. Get your friends to clap their hands rhythmically while you perform these moves as dramatically as you can.

1. Stand as tall as you can. Reach up with your right arm and pretend you're plucking an apple from a high branch of a tree. Hold the imaginary apple with the very tips of your fingers.

2. Now you must pretend you are going to take a bite from the apple. Rotate your wrist clockwise as you bend your elbow and bring your imaginary apple towards your mouth (don't actually bite).

3. Now start swinging your hips, stomping your feet and turning in circles.

4. Pretend to throw the apple to the ground, a look of utter disgust on your face.

5. Now stamp on the imaginary apple, moving your feet faster and faster as you crush it to a pulp.

6. Repeat.

HOW TO EAT SPAGHETTI LIKE A REAL ITALIAN

Forget about cutting up your spaghetti or fiddling with spoons – all real Italians need is a fork and a little know-how.

1. Poke the prongs of the fork into the spaghetti and scoop up a small amount. Lift it high off the plate to release it from the rest of the spaghetti and to allow any stray strands to fall. If you've taken too much, now's the time to wiggle the fork slightly and let some excess fall off.

2. Look for an area of the plate that's food-free. Quickly point the prongs of the fork straight down onto it.

3. Twirl the fork a few times to create a roll of strands.

4. Quickly flick your wrist and place the rolled-up spaghetti into your mouth. *Bravo!*

HOW TO DRESS TO SUIT YOUR STAR SIGN

Each star sign is said to have its own special fashion style. Check out the looks linked to your star sign and see if it sounds like you.

ARIES – MARCH 21ST TO APRIL 20TH

You're a trend-setter – always willing to try new looks. You've got brilliant fashion radar and you know whether an outfit's going to become a hit or a miss. Your favourite colours are red and black.

TAURUS – APRIL 21ST TO MAY 21ST

You'd rather snap up a vintage cashmere jumper for a few pounds than spend the same amount on a cheap high-street T-shirt. You love subtle, expensive shades of brown, khaki and cream.

GEMINI – MAY 22ND TO JUNE 21ST

You get bored hanging on to any outfit for too long. You mix and match styles and love shimmery fabrics and coloured patterns.

CANCER – JUNE 22ND TO JULY 23RD

You love comfortable, feminine clothes – soft jumpers and floaty skirts. If you find a piece of clothing you like, you keep it in your wardrobe for years. You love to dress in soft blues and greens.

LEO – JULY 24TH TO AUGUST 23RD

You wear anything that makes a statement – from flowing tops to nipped-in jackets. You love gold, red, bronze and orange.

VIRGO – AUGUST 24TH TO SEPTEMBER 23RD

Virgo is the best-turned-out star sign of all – you'll spend a lot of time taking care of your clothes. You love neat and tidy looks and soft fabrics with natural colours like green, grey and brown.

LIBRA – SEPTEMBER 24TH TO OCTOBER 23RD

You've got great taste and favour classical looks. Somehow, though, you always manage to put an outfit together that looks up-to-date and modern. You opt for rich blues, dark pinks and black.

SCORPIO – OCTOBER 24TH TO NOVEMBER 22ND

One day you're super-smart, the next barefoot and natural – a real mixture. The colours you keep coming back to are black and red.

SAGITTARIUS – NOVEMBER 23RD TO DECEMBER 21ST

You love colourful, casual clothes that let you move, and you don't really care what others think of you. You prefer soft, natural fibres in earthy shades of purple, green and dark blue.

CAPRICORN – DECEMBER 22ND TO JANUARY 20TH

You're not a label snob – as long as you like an outfit, you don't care how much it costs or what range it comes from. Colour-wise, you favour charcoal grey, brown and black.

AQUARIUS – JANUARY 21ST TO FEBRUARY 19TH

You're unconventional with clothes and your friends often look to you for a hint of what style might be in next. You experiment with colour but always find yourself coming back to blue.

PISCES – FEBRUARY 20TH TO MARCH 20TH

You would happily buy all your clothes from a second-hand shop but when you dress up you can look as good as anyone. Your favourite colours are silver, purple and cream.

HOW TO WALK IN HIGH-HEELED SHOES

High-heeled shoes look lovely if you're off to a party or a wedding but they can be tricky to walk in at first. Follow this simple guide and you'll soon be skipping around like a real lady.

• Choose a low heel or a wedge (where the gap between the heel and toe is filled in) so that you can practise walking more easily – don't aim too high at first.

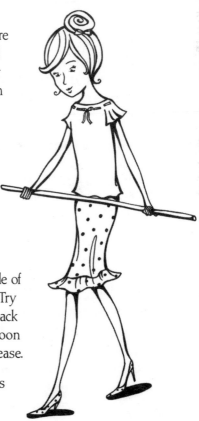

• Find a good place to practise where you have plenty to hold on to and stand up slowly and carefully. Your centre of gravity will be higher than usual so flex each knee a little to steady yourself.

• Keep your bottom tucked in and balance on the balls of your feet. Take a few steps placing each heel first before putting your toe down. Be careful not to get a heel caught in the carpet.

• Keep practising at home for a couple of days until you feel ready to go out. Try a short trip around the corner and back before attempting a longer outing. Soon you'll be able to run for a bus with ease.

Top tip. Take a spare pair of flat shoes along, too, just in case you get tired.

HOW TO FIND THE PERFECT PERFUME

There are thousands of perfumes in the shops, which means it can be hard to whittle them down to find the one you really like and which most suits your personality.

TRIAL AND ERROR

• Head for the perfume counter at a department store or a large chemist for the best choice. Try a maximum of three – your nose will get tired and they will all start to smell the same.

• Start by taking a look at the ingredients before you spritz. If you're quite girly you might love floral perfumes. If you're sporty, citrus scents like lemon or grapefruit could be ideal.

• Spray a little onto the inside of your wrist or elbow, then wait ten minutes for the perfume to 'develop' properly. You shouldn't buy a perfume even if you like it straight away. Perfumes often smell quite different after a couple of hours. If you like the way it smells on your skin later on in the day, you're on to a winner.

HOW TO WEAR IT

The best place to wear a perfume is on one of your pulse points – where the blood is closest to your skin's surface. These include your temples, the side of your neck (not behind your ears!), in the crook of your elbow, your inner wrists, the backs of your knees and on the front of your ankles. Some perfumers recommend spritzing freshly washed hair so that you waft a delicious scent around you as you move your head.

HOW TO MAKE A MOOD BOARD

The most glamorous girls always know what suits them, as well as the styles and colours they really love. You can work out your own personal style, too, by creating a 'Mood Board' for your bedroom.

First of all, you'll need a pin board for the wall. If you haven't got one of these, try securing four cork floor tiles to your wall with sticky tac.

Now the fun bit... start collecting clippings from fashion magazines, photos, old postcards, adverts, paint swatches, fabric scraps, leaves – anything at all. The only important thing is that you really love everything. Take your time deciding which things really appeal to you. Spread them out on your bed while you decide. You may be able to gather them into little sections of similar colours or style.

Once you're happy with your selection, arrange them onto your pin board. Now sit back and take a look – your personal taste will be there for you to admire whenever you want.

HOW TO SEEM CONFIDENT WHEN YOU'RE NOT

The next time you're feeling shy and overwhelmed, try out these DOs and DON'Ts to make others think you're feeling completely confident...

• DON'T wear dull colours.
Instead of trying to blend in with the background, get yourself noticed by wearing confident reds, oranges or yellows.

• DO get your body language right.
Hold your head high however nervous you feel. Don't clasp your hands in front of you or fold them – it's much better to stand with your arms hanging relaxed and loose at your sides. Sit with your hands resting loosely in your lap.

• DON'T hide behind your hair.
Let people see your face – hair swept back into a neat ponytail says that you're okay about people looking at you.

• DO smile.
People often confuse shyness with unfriendliness – a smile shows you're friendly and makes people feel relaxed around you.

• DON'T talk too quickly.
Relax and take a deep breath. Take your time and give yourself a chance to think about what you want to say. Avoid just blurting out the first thing that comes into your head.

• DO look people in the eye.
One of the most obvious signs of shyness is when you avoid making eye contact with the person you're talking to.

• DON'T chew your nails.
Nibbling on fingers is a dead give-away that you're feeling nervous.

• DO lift your spirits with scent.
Apply a dot of grapefruit or bergamot essential oil on your wrists before heading out the door in the morning. They're great for boosting your confidence and you can take a quick sniff whenever you need a boost.

HOW TO STRIKE A POSE

When everyone is looking your way it's vital to make sure that your every move seems as naturally glamorous as possible, whether you've just popped to the corner shop or you're making a brief appearance at a film premier. Next time you're on the red carpet try out these top moves.

THE HAIR FLIP

As you step onto the school bus smile, wave and flip your head up so that your hair swishes out behind you. Try not to catch yourself in the eye though, as this will sting.

THE LOOK BEHIND YOU

Walk past your waiting photographers without stopping. Just when they think you've ignored them completely stop, put one hand on your hip and look back over your shoulder before giving them your best smile.

THE BIG TUMBLE

This one is usually best avoided but it's important to be prepared so that you can gracefully jump straight back up again if you fall.

Now practise, practise, practise...

HOW TO EMPHASISE YOUR EYE COLOUR

A great way to make your natural eye colour really stand out for parties is to wear clothes in just the right shade. Forget about wearing blues if you have blue eyes, and browns if you have brown eyes – these are the best choices...

Eye Colour: pale blue
Try: lilac or pastel pink

Eye Colour: mid-to-dark blue
Try: peach or gold

Eye Colour: light brown
Try: honey brown or khaki green

Eye Colour: dark brown
Try: toffee brown or olive green

Eye Colour: pale green
Try: lavender or blue-grey

Eye Colour: dark green
Try: peach or plum

Eye Colour: hazel
Try: moss green or purple.

HOW TO BEAD YOUR HAIR

Beaded hair looks really pretty and costs just pennies. It only takes a little time and practice to achieve.

You'll need:

• A handful of beads with large holes. Plastic ones are best as they're lighter – you don't want to be too weighed down.

• A reel of cotton, any colour.

How to do it:

1. Pick up a strand of hair about the thickness of a shoelace.

2. Divide it into three smaller strands.

3. Plait the three strands together until you have about 5 cm of hair left at the ends.

4. Wet the end of the plait and smooth the ends together.

5. Thread a bead onto the plait and push it up the hair.

6. Add as many beads as you like, carefully pushing each one up the plait.

7. When you've finished, wind a length of cotton around the

end of the plait and tie in place. Alternatively, use
a thin hairband, if you prefer.

8. Repeat the whole process to make as many plaits
as you like. You could even enlist some friends
to help you bead all of your hair.

HOW TO TELL WHAT THE SHAPE OF YOUR LIPSTICK MEANS

Raid your friends' make-up bags, whip out their used lipsticks or
lipbalms and explain how the shape of the tip reveals loads about
their personalities.

FLAT TOP

You're dependable and don't mess around. You care what people
think about you.

CONCAVE TOP

This bowl-shape means you're friendly, exciting and love a dare.

SLANTED TOP

If the end is close to its original shape, you probably stick to the
rules and don't like too much attention.

ROUNDED TOP

You're a loveable, friendly person who enjoys being busy.

POINTED TOP

You're kind and easygoing and can be relied on in a crisis.

HOW TO LOOK AFTER YOUR SKIN IN SUMMER

Everyone loves a day at the beach in Summer – but no one likes getting burnt by the sun. Check out this safe tan plan.

• Apply suntan lotion (SPF 15 or higher) first thing in the morning before getting dressed – that way you won't miss any areas.

• Lips are especially prone to burning and chapping in the sun – so slick on some lip salve.

• Stay out of the sun between 12 noon and 3 o'clock when the sun is at its hottest. Move into the shade or cover up with a T-shirt and a broad-brimmed hat.

• If you're a sporty type or fancy a cooling dip in the sea, choose a special waterproof sun lotion.

HOW TO LOOK AFTER YOUR SKIN IN WINTER

• Chilly temperatures and cold winds can make your skin dry and itchy. Always protect yourself with warm mittens, cosy scarves and cute hats.

• Dress in layers that will keep you warm from top to toe. Light cotton next to the skin helps keep your skin warm and dry.

• Bathe or shower in lukewarm water. Hot baths may sound nice but the heat can dry out the natural oils in your skin making it even itchier than before.

• Don't lick sore lips to try and soothe them, you'll make them even flakier. Slick on some balm or petroleum jelly instead.

HOW TO ESCAPE
A HORDE OF FANS

It's difficult to be polite and glamorous all the time, so if you just need some time to yourself use these top tips to get away from the crowds.

• Kit yourself out with a brilliant disguise.
A wig and dark glasses are a great way to start but don't go overboard. A wooden leg and a parrot will only draw more attention to you.

• Get to know your route home like the back of your hand. Try to plan a clever detour and give everyone the slip when they least expect it.

• Perfect your celebrity-style wave. It's best performed getting into of an expensive car, but the school bus will do at a pinch. Walk quickly with your head down. Just before you get on, stop and turn to face your 'fans'. Raise your arm briefly and flash a quick smile. Remember – the more excited your fans are, the more disinterested your wave should be. Now turn and enter the bus, refusing, all autographs.

• Come up with a false name – the name of your favourite cartoon combined with your first pet is a simple way of doing this. Use it whenever you travel to avoid detection.

• If you find your exit blocked by autograph-hunters at your local café politely ask the owner if you can go through the kitchen instead and leave via the back door.

HOW TO TAKE CHARGE OF OUT-OF-CONTROL HAIR

The weather can wreak havoc on your hair. If your pretty curls have a case of the frizzies, or fly-away static is ruining your lovely tresses, try these helpful hints to take your hair in hand:

- **Frizzy.** Use a conditioner each time you wash your hair to keep it as sleek as possible – save lots of time with a spray-on and leave-in brand.

- **Frizzy.** Use your fingers as styling tools instead of brushes and combs – you're less likely to create frizz.

- **Frizzy.** Rub a few drops of almond oil between your palms, then smooth over your hair to combat crazy curls.

- **Fly-away.** Dry winter air can literally make your hair stand on end – use a wooden brush to help reduce static electricity.

- **Fly-away.** Use a moisturising shampoo and conditioner to stop your hair drying out.

- **Fly-away.** Spritz anti-static hairspray onto your brush before styling your hair.

125

HOW TO CHOOSE THE RIGHT SUNGLASSES FOR YOUR FACE SHAPE

Choosing the right pair of shades to suit your face shape can transform your whole look and give you just the right finishing touch. Check out how to work out your face shape on page 40, then decide which frames would suit you the best.

ROUND-SHAPED FACE

Look for broad styles which are equal to the width of your face. Square lenses look good, too.

HEART-SHAPED FACE

Delicate or rimless frames suit your pretty face shape perfectly. Angular shapes are also a good choice for you.

SQUARE-SHAPED FACE

Soft, gently curved, oval-shaped frames soften your defined features perfectly.

OVAL-SHAPED FACE

Lucky thing – everything suits you!

HOW TO BE A GODDESS

Owing to the goddess-like status you have now achieved by reading this book, you'll need to learn how to cope with the stresses and strains this role may bring.

• If you really want to look like a goddess borrow an old, white sheet and drape it around yourself in the style of a Roman toga.

• Wind some pretty flowers through your hair and always remember to leave a trail of blossoms wherever you walk.

• Smile gently at all times to give people the impression that you're calm and serene.

• If people are nice enough to offer you gifts, do your best to accept them with good manners (even if you'd rather they hadn't bothered).

• One of the best goddess skills you will learn is wisdom. Use it well and try to give the best advice you can.

• Most importantly – never abuse your powers.

ALSO AVAILABLE...

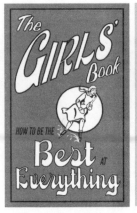

The Girls' Book: How To
Be The Best At Everything
ISBN: 978-1-905158-79-9

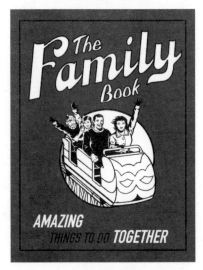

The Boys' Book of Survival:
How To Survive
Anything, Anywhere
ISBN: 978-1-906082-12-3

The Boys' Book: How To
Be The Best At Everything
ISBN: 978-1-905158-64-5

The Family Book:
Amazing Things To Do Together
ISBN: 978-1-906082-10-9

Was gibt es Schöneres, als unverhofft auf die große Liebe zu stoßen? Oder auf ungeahnte Lesefreuden?

Über das große Glück, das zu finden, wonach man nicht gesucht hat, schreibt Mark Forsyth in seinem charmanten und witzigen Essay, der zugleich eine Liebeserklärung an die gute Buchhandlung ist. Denn nur dort kann man zufällig genau das Buch entdecken, von dem man noch gar nicht wusste, wie sehr man es lieben wird.

Felicitas von Lovenberg hat bekannte Autorinnen und Autoren gefragt, welche Momente sie mit Buchhandlungen verbinden, und diese Geschichten vom Glück, das in Büchern steckt, hier versammelt.

Felicitas von Lovenberg, Jahrgang 1974, war von 1998 bis 2016 Redakteurin im Feuilleton der »Frankfurter Allgemeinen Zeitung«, dort seit 2001 in der Literaturredaktion, die sie seit 2008 leitet. Sie wurde ausgezeichnet mit dem Alfred-Kerr-Preis für Literaturkritik, dem Ernst-Robert-Curtius-Förderpreis für Essayistik, dem Hildegard-von-Bingen-Preis für Publizistik und dem Julius-Campe-Preis für Kritik. Im SWR-Fernsehen moderierte sie regelmäßig die Literatursendung »lesenswert«.

Seit 2016 ist Felicitas von Lovenberg Verlegerin des Piper Verlags.

Weitere Informationen finden Sie auf www.fischerverlage.de

DER GUTEN
BUCHHANDLUNG

Herausgegeben von
Felicitas von Lovenberg

FISCHER Taschenbuch

Aus Verantwortung für die Umwelt hat sich der S. Fischer Verlag zu einer nachhaltigen Buchproduktion verpflichtet. Der bewusste Umgang mit unseren Ressourcen, der Schutz unseres Klimas und der Natur gehören zu unseren obersten Unternehmenszielen.

Gemeinsam mit unseren Partnern und Lieferanten setzen wir uns für eine klimaneutrale Buchproduktion ein, die den Erwerb von Klimazertifikaten zur Kompensation des CO_2-Ausstoßes einschließt.

Weitere Informationen finden Sie unter: www.klimaneutralerverlag.de

2. Auflage: April 2020

Erschienen bei FISCHER Taschenbuch
Frankfurt am Main, April 2020

Für den Text von Mark Forsyth:
Die Originalausgabe erschien unter dem Titel
»The Unknown Unknown. Bookshops And
The Delight Of Not Getting What You Want«
im Verlag Icon Books, London
© 2014 Mark Forsyth

Die deutschsprachige Ausgabe des Textes
von Mark Forsyth erschien unter dem Titel
»Lob der guten Buchhandlung oder Vom Glück,
das zu finden, wonach Sie gar nicht gesucht haben«
© 2015 S. Fischer Verlag GmbH, Hedderichstr. 114,
D-60596 Frankfurt am Main

Für alle weiteren Texte:
© 2020 S. Fischer Verlag GmbH, Hedderichstr. 114,
D-60596 Frankfurt am Main

Satz: Dörlemann Satz, Lemförde
Druck und Bindung: CPI books GmbH, Leck
Printed in Germany
ISBN 978-3-596-70543-6

INHALT

FELICITAS
VON LOVENBERG

Vorwort

Es gibt ein wunderbares Lied von Frank Sinatra Junior, dessen Stimme übrigens exakt so klingt wie die seines ungleich berühmteren Vaters, das mir unwillkürlich jedes Mal einfällt, wenn ich eine Buchhandlung betrete. Das Lied heißt »The People That You Never Get To Love«. Es beschwört jene flüchtigen Begegnungen, in denen sich Blicke treffen und wo für einen winzigen Moment eine Möglichkeit aufblitzt, bevor man den Eindruck abschüttelt, zusammen mit der leisen Wehmut über die verpasste Gelegenheit. Es sind diese Was-wäre-wenn-Momente, in denen man sich ausmalt, wie man die Person, die da gerade vor uns in den Aufzug oder in die S-Bahn steigt, aufhalten könnte – und wie sich dadurch der ganze Verlauf unserer beider Geschichte verändern würde.

Das von Rupert Holmes in den späten Siebzigern komponierte Lied hebt an mit folgender Szene:

You're browsing through a second hand bookstore
And you see her in non-fiction V through Y

She looks up from World War II
And then you catch her, catching you catching her
  eye

And you quickly turn away your wishful stare
And take a sudden interest in your shoes
If you only had the courage but you don't
She turns and leaves and you both lose

Diese Szene der verpassten romantischen Chance hat einiges gemein mit Mark Forsyths virtuosem Aufsatz »Lob der guten Buchhandlung«, dem dieses Buch nicht nur seinen Titel, sondern auch die Inspiration verdankt. Der englische Etymologe und Sprachliebhaber Forsyth schreibt in diesem scharfsinnigen Stück, das Sie am besten jetzt sofort lesen, damit Sie nie wieder ein Leben führen, in dem Sie diesen Essay nicht kannten – Forsyth also schreibt darin von dem Glück, Bücher zu finden, die man dringend braucht, obwohl man zuvor gar nicht nach ihnen gesucht hatte – aus dem einfachen Grund, weil man nicht wusste, dass sie überhaupt existieren. »Wo sind sie? Wer sind sie? Ich habe absolut keine Ahnung. Wahrscheinlich feiern sie nebenan eine Party ... Aber ich bin nicht eingeladen. Und ich kann es ihnen noch nicht einmal vorwerfen. Wir sind uns nie begegnet. Und ich kann sie nicht finden, weil ich ihre Namen nicht kenne. Sie sind die unbekannten Unbekannten, und ich kann mich noch nicht einmal nach ihnen verzehren, so groß ist meine doppelte Unkenntnis.« Die Liebe zu den Büchern, die wir nicht kennen, weil wir nicht von ihnen wissen, mag etwas weniger konjunktivisch veranlagt sein als die zu den Menschen, in die wir uns niemals verlieben, weil wir nie ihre Bekanntschaft machen. Aber nur ein wenig.

Moment, bewegen wir uns hier nicht im Reich der unendlichen Möglichkeiten und Kombinationen? Und versprechen nicht Algorithmen hier eine hohe Treffsicherheit? Keineswegs. Für Forsyth ist das Internet für das Finden des richtigen Buches für den richtigen Leser etwa so nützlich wie Speed-Dating-Webseiten für die Epiphanie der wahren Liebe, nämlich gar nicht. Denn »Maschinen lassen dem Zufall keine Chance. Sie tun genau das, was man ihnen sagt. Darum wird man im Internet nichts anderes bekommen als das, wovon man schon wusste, dass man es wollte.«

Tatsächlich ist die Wahrscheinlichkeit, etwas zu finden, von dem man zuvor nicht einmal wusste, dass es existiert, und das sich als wichtig für die eigene Lesebiographie entpuppt, nirgends größer als in der guten Buchhandlung, die zum Stöbern einlädt und verführt durch die Darbietung und die vom Buchhändler mit Verstand und Leidenschaft kuratierte Auswahl der unbekannten Bücher.

Die Marktforschung hantiert gern mit dem Begriff des »Zielkaufs«. Der Kunde kommt in eine Buchhandlung, weil er ein ganz bestimmtes Buch haben möchte. Hält man es mit den Konsumentenforschern, tun sich nun zwei Szenarien auf. Ist der Titel vorrätig, kauft unser Kunde ihn und geht wieder. Ist er nicht vorrätig, geht er auch und kauft ihn woanders. In meiner Vorstellung spielt sich diese Geschichte ganz anders ab. Vielleicht beginnt sie tatsächlich damit, dass jemand ein bestimmtes Buch kaufen möchte, das ihm jemand empfohlen hat oder auf das er durch eine Rezension aufmerksam geworden ist. Er betritt die Buchhandlung seiner Wahl. Sobald er die Schwelle überschreitet, befindet er sich in einer anderen Welt. Der Lärm des Alltags rauscht etwas leiser, und Zeit meint plötzlich nicht nur Zukunft, sondern Gegenwart. Unmittelbar umfängt ihn der Zauber, der von den einladend mit Büchern bestückten Tischen aufsteigt und aus den Regalen quillt, diese immer wieder neue und doch jedem Leser vertraute Atmosphäre der versammelten Geschichten und Gedanken, Ideen und Erkenntnisse, Hoffnungen und Thesen, eben das leise Murmeln geistiger Zwiegespräche, die gute Buchhandlungen mit exquisiten Bibliotheken gemein haben.

Bedürfnisse müssen geweckt werden, bevor man ihnen nachgehen kann. Darum ist die Umgebung so entscheidend für Entdeckungen. Manche meiner schönsten Buchkäufe verdanke ich der Beobachtung anderer Kunden in der Buchhandlung. Einmal stand ich bei Blackwell's in Bristol, offiziell, weil ich bestimmte Bücher fürs Studium brauchte. Wie so oft hielt ich mich zunächst im Belletristikbereich auf, als eine sehr apart aussehende Dame hereinstürmte und ihren Blick ungeduldig über die Auslage schweifen ließ, bevor sie sich, offenkundig fündig geworden, einen ganzen Stapel eines Buches schnappte und damit zur Kasse marschierte, wo sie den Turm ablegte und mit hörbarer Empörung in der Stimme fragte: »Is that all you've got?« Die erschrockene Buchhändlerin versicherte, man könne natürlich umgehend für Nachschub sorgen, aber ein paar Tage – wir schrieben das Jahr

1994 – werde es wohl dauern, bis »Captain Corelli's Mandolin« von Louis de Bernières wieder vorrätig sei. Dann solle man ihr bitte gleich zehn weitere Exemplare reservieren, sagte die Dame, denn sie habe die Absicht, den Roman all ihren Freunden zu schenken. Zu einer anderen Lieblingslektüre kam ich durch den Blackwell's Children Bookshop in Oxford, in dem ich während des Studiums gern stundenlang Zeit verbrachte. Überhaupt erst aufmerksam auf diese spezielle Blackwell's-Filiale – Oxford war damals voll davon – wurde ich durch einen in der Auslage baumelnden Reisigbesen. Das gerade erschienene Buch, von dem mir die Buchhändlerin dann vorschwärmte, hieß »Harry Potter und der Stein der Weisen«.

Doch nicht für alle unsere wesentlichen Buchkäufe gibt es so eindeutige Erklärungen und Wegweiser. Oft genug ist es etwas Unbewusstes, das uns anzieht und uns zu diesem und nicht zu jenem Buch greifen lässt. Für mich haben diese geradezu instinktiven Entscheidungen etwas Magisches, das die Lektüre besonders auflädt. Auch Forsyth schildert die beglückte Verblüffung über solche Buchkäufe: »Ich habe mich nie besonders für Science-Fiction erwärmen können. Ich mag Science und ich mag Fiction. Aber eben getrennt voneinander. Deshalb weiß ich auch nicht, warum ich eines Tages einen Roman von Philip K. Dick in die Hand nahm. Die einzige Erklärung dafür ist, dass er auf einem Tisch in der Buchhandlung lag. Mir gefiel die erste Seite. Mit gefiel die zweite Seite. Und als ich auf Seite 10 angekommen war, wurde mir klar, dass ich das Buch unbedingt kaufen musste. Nachdem ich es ausgelesen hatte, wollte ich mehr. Dringend.«

Ah, die herrliche und folgenschwere Kombination von der Lust am Lesen und einem kleinen Kaufrausch! Denn so schön es ist, in Buchhandlungen zu stöbern – irgendwann will man seine Beute doch nach Hause schleppen, wo man sich in eine ruhige Ecke verziehen und loslesen kann. Als ich noch klein war und dem Zauber des Lesens erst frisch verfallen, traf mein Vater eine folgenschwere Vereinbarung mit mir. Für Bücher, die ich lesen wollte, würde es immer genug Taschengeld geben – vorausgesetzt, sie bestanden seine durchaus strenge väterliche Qualitätskontrolle. Bücher, das machte er mir damit klar, sind Lebensmittel und keine Luxusgüter. Das sollte ihn teuer zu stehen kommen, denn von Büchern konnte ich damals schon so wenig genug bekommen wie heute. Heute weiß ich, was für ein Geschenk es war, dass ich noch nie erst auf Weihnachten oder meinen Geburtstag warten musste, um an neuen Lesestoff zu kommen, sondern durfte meine Mutter häufig in die Stadt begleiten, wo sie mich getrost in der Buchhandlung absetzen und Stunden später wieder abholen konnte. Mit mir verließ immer ein Stapel Bücher den Laden.

Überhaupt: Zeit. Sie ist die vielleicht unschätzbarste Zutat des Zaubers einer guten Buchhandlung. Dort scheinen die Uhren anders zu ticken als sonst. Denn fürs richtige Stöbern braucht man Zeit – und niemand weiß besser als Buchhändler, dass die Kunst der Muße mehr und mehr ins Hintertreffen geraten ist. Wer sich aber Zeit nimmt, ob eine Viertelstunde, eine kleine Weile oder gar, wie Ilija Trojanow, eine ganze Nacht in der Buchhandlung seiner Wahl verbringt, der begegnet nicht nur Neuem, sondern schließlich sogar sich selbst. Jedenfalls bekommt man die Zeit, die man in einer Buchhandlung verbringt, immer doppelt und dreifach zurück.

Angesichts der Tatsache, dass es ausschließlich Schriftsteller sind, die hier zum Lob der guten Buchhandlung versammelt sind, mag man fragen, wie objektiv ausgerechnet diese sein können, wenn es um den Ort geht, an dem nicht zuletzt ihre eigenen Erzeugnisse verkauft werden. Bezeichnenderweise beschreibt keiner der Autoren das Glück, das eigene Buch in einer Buchhandlung wiederzufinden, ob auf dem (häufig erwähnten) Tisch mit den ausgewählten Neuerscheinungen oder etwas versteckter einsortiert im Regal. Ebenfalls keine Erwähnung findet die Buchhandlung als Ort der schriftstellerischen Arbeit, von Lesungen und der Begegnung mit dem Publikum. Der Grund dafür ist so einfach, dass man ihn glatt übersehen könnte: Buchhandlungen sind Geburtsorte von Literatur. Kaum ein Autor, der nicht als Leser begonnen und schon im Kindesalter davon geträumt hätte, sich selbst in Buchform unter den Giganten zu tummeln, Rücken an Rücken zu stehen oder zu liegen mit den eigenen Lieblingsbüchern, bestaunt von Lesern wie ihm selbst.

Doch Buchhandlungen sind nicht nur dazu da, unsere geistigen Bedürfnisse zu erfüllen, sondern auch dazu, diese immer weiter zu verfeinern und zu vervielfältigen. Jede Entscheidung für ein Buch ist auch eine Entscheidung gegen unzählige andere, die jetzt noch nicht dran sein können oder nie dran sein werden. Die Fähigkeit des einzelnen Buches, zu seinem Leser zu sprechen, als habe es seine Botschaft genau für ihn und genau für diesen Moment bewahrt, gehört zu den immer wieder frappierenden Lese-Erlebnissen. In guten Buchhandlungen finden wir darum nicht nur etwas, von dem wir zuvor gar nicht wussten, wie dringend wir es brauchen. Sondern sie lassen uns auch spüren, dass wir noch etwas brauchen, etwas, von dem wir noch gar nicht wissen, was es ist. Die gute Buchhandlung schickt uns darum stets beglückt, aber zugleich auch etwas sehnsüchtig wieder hinaus in die Welt. Wir werden bald zurückkehren, um das Verpasste doch noch zu erwischen.

MARK FORSYTH

Lob der guten Buchhandlung
oder
Vom Glück, das zu finden,
wonach Sie gar nicht gesucht haben

Unbekanntes Unbekanntes

Meine Ansichten über Buchhandlungen verdanke ich nicht unwesentlich Donald Rumsfeld. Falls Sie vergessen haben oder nicht wissen sollten, wer das ist: Donald Rumsfeld war der amerikanische Verteidigungsminister unter Gerald Ford und George Bush dem Jüngeren. Ihm wird mitunter vorgeworfen, unnötig Kriege angezettelt zu haben, zu glauben, er stehe über dem Völkerrecht, und sich mehr für Origami als für Menschenleben zu interessieren. Das ist aber noch nicht alles, was er und ich gemeinsam haben. Vor allem sein Glaube an die Notwendigkeit von Buchhandlungen ist es, der uns eint:

»Es gibt Dinge, von denen wir wissen, dass wir sie wissen. Es gibt bekanntes Unbekanntes, also Dinge, von denen wir wissen, dass wir sie nicht wissen. Aber es gibt auch unbekanntes Unbekanntes. Es gibt Dinge, von denen wir nicht wissen, dass wir sie nicht wissen.«

Ich werde wohl nie nachvollziehen können, warum manche das merkwürdig finden und sich darüber lustig machen. Eine Sprachgesellschaft verlieh Mr Rumsfeld sogar ihren »Fettnäpfchen-Preis des Jahres« für die »wirrste Äußerung einer öffentlichen Person«. Aber in Wirklichkeit ist gar nichts wirr daran. Ich weiß, dass Paris die Hauptstadt von Frankreich ist, aber vor allem *weiß* ich, dass ich weiß, dass Paris die Hauptstadt von Frankreich ist. Ich weiß, dass ich *nicht* weiß, was die Hauptstadt von Aserbaidschan ist, obwohl ich mir nicht sicher bin, dass Aserbaidschan überhaupt eine Hauptstadt hat. Das gehört zu den Dingen, die ich einmal nachschlagen sollte. Aber ich weiß nicht … tja, jetzt wird es kompliziert. Sie wissen nicht, dass Sie nicht wissen, was die Hauptstadt von Erewhon[1] ist, weil Sie keine Ahnung hatten, dass es überhaupt ein Land namens Erewhon gibt, und deshalb hatten Sie auch keine Ahnung, dass Sie eine Wissenslücke haben. Sie wussten nicht, dass Sie das nicht wussten.

1 *Erewhon* ist der Titel eines Romans von Samuel Butler aus dem Jahr 1872, der in einem fiktiven Land dieses Namens spielt; es handelt sich um ein Anagramm des Wortes ›Nowhere‹, englisch für ›Nirgendwo‹ bzw. ›Utopia‹. (A.d.Ü.)

Dasselbe gilt für Bücher. Ich weiß, dass ich *Große Erwartungen* gelesen habe. Das ist etwas bekanntes Bekanntes. Ich weiß, dass ich nicht *Krieg und Frieden* gelesen habe. Das ist, für mich, etwas bekanntes Unbekanntes (und falls ich keine lange Haftstrafe antreten muss, wird das wohl auch so bleiben). Aber es gibt Bücher, von denen ich noch nie gehört habe. Und weil ich nie von ihnen gehört habe, habe ich keine Ahnung, dass ich sie nicht gelesen habe.

Ich würde liebend gerne eines dieser Bücher aufzählen, von denen ich nie gehört habe. Ich würde Ihnen gerne ein Beispiel nennen, aber sehen Sie: Ich kann es nicht, weil ich nie von ihnen gehört habe. Tolstoi, Stendhal, Cervantes, diese Männer verfolgen mich immerzu. Sie stehen in dunklen Ecken herum und schauen mich missbilligend mit hochgezogenen Augenbrauen an. Und all das nur, weil ich nie dazu gekommen bin, ihre verfluchten, tonnenschweren, staatstragenden, tausendseitigen Fünf-Generationen-Schinken zu lesen. Ist mir doch egal. Meistens jedenfalls. Manchmal fällt mir wieder ein, dass ich so langsam wie eine Schildkröte lese und dass es um die Ecke eine Kneipe gibt. Zum Teufel mit Tolstoi, sage ich, und ich sage es im vollen Bewusstsein um seine grenzenlose Bedeutung und seinen langen Bart.

Aber die anderen. Wo sind sie? Wer sind sie? Ich habe absolut keine Ahnung. Wahrscheinlich feiern sie nebenan eine Party. Und was für eine, mit wunderschönen Weinen und köstlichen Frauen. Aber ich bin nicht eingeladen. Und ich kann es ihnen noch nicht einmal vorwerfen. Wir sind uns nie begegnet. Und ich kann sie nicht finden, weil ich ihre Namen nicht kenne. Sie sind die unbekannten Unbekannten, und ich kann mich noch nicht einmal nach ihnen verzehren, so groß ist meine doppelte Unkenntnis.

Und deshalb und darum die Buchhandlung. Auch wenn es hier und da hieß, Mr Rumsfeld habe tatsächlich über mesopotamische Waffenkunst gesprochen – natürlich meinte er die verschiedenen Arten, Bücher zu kaufen. Wir alle werden manchmal ein wenig missverstanden.

Es gibt, wie er sagte, drei verschiedene Typen von Büchern: Die, die wir gelesen haben, die, von denen wir wissen, dass wir sie noch nicht gelesen haben (wie *Krieg und Frieden*), und die anderen: die Bücher, von denen wir nicht wissen, dass wir sie nicht kennen.

Diejenigen, die Sie gelesen haben, brauchen Sie nicht zu kaufen. Vermutlich haben Sie ein Exemplar erstanden (oder geklaut), bevor Sie es gelesen haben. Die berühmten Bücher, die Sie nicht gelesen haben – also die bekannten Unbekannten –, sind leicht zu bekommen: Es gibt sie im Internet. Sie tippen »Krieg und Frieden« in Ihren Computer ein, und alle möglichen Internethändler werden anbieten, Ihnen das Buch für einen Appel und ein Ei zu verkaufen und es Ihnen obendrein noch heute zum Kaffee persönlich vorbeizubringen.

Vermutlich wäre dies die geeignete Stelle, um über die modernen Zeiten zu klagen, und darüber, wie wir allmählich den Kontakt zu anderen Menschen verlieren und unaufhaltsam auf den Abgrund zusteuern – aber das kann ich nicht. Das Internet ist viel zu komfortabel. Vielleicht war das Leben deutlich gesünder, als alles noch von Menschenhand erledigt wurde. Aber es dauerte auch alles viel länger. Außerdem kann man diese Leier der falschen Nostalgie unendlich drehen. Die Menschen fanden es furchtbar, als Taschenbücher auf den Markt kamen, und nannten sie abfällig Groschenhefte. Ich vermute, das war auch nicht anders, als Johannes Gutenberg im 15. Jahrhundert die Druckpresse erfand:

Die Klöster waren voller Mönche, die glaubten, einer *gedruckten* Bibel fehle das Menschliche. Wahrscheinlich könnte man zurück ins Jahr 3000 v. Chr. reisen, nur um dort einem Ägypter zu begegnen, der sich darüber beklagt, dass die hübschen Hieroglyphen von der hypermodernen hieratischen Schrift verdrängt worden seien. Es hört einfach nie auf.

Die Welt hat sich weitergedreht, und alles Mögliche ist im ewigen Dunkel der Geschichte verschwunden – Dampfmaschinen, Hörkassetten und die Pocken. Sosehr wir das beklagen mögen, wir wollen das alles nicht wirklich wiederhaben. Das Internet ist eine großartige Erfindung, die uns erhalten bleiben wird. Wenn Sie etwas wissen wollen, das Internet wird es für Sie finden. Mein persönliches Anliegen und das ganze Anliegen dieses Essays ist Folgendes: Es genügt nicht, etwas zu bekommen, von dem man schon weiß, dass man es wollte. Die besten Sachen sind die, von denen Sie gar nicht wussten, dass Sie sie wollten, bis Sie sie bekommen haben.

Das Internet verschluckt Ihre Bedürfnisse und spuckt sie verdaut wieder aus. Sie suchen, Sie geben Begriffe ein, die Sie kennen, Dinge, die Sie schon im Kopf haben, und das Internet bietet Ihnen ein Buch oder ein Bild oder einen Wikipedia-Artikel an. Aber das ist auch alles. Das unbekannte Unbekannte müssen wir woanders finden.

Seltsame Bücher

Ich bin der stolze Besitzer einer merkwürdigen literarischen Rarität: »Fiktion voran: Eine Anthologie mit Kurzgeschichten der Mitarbeiter von First-Bus«, einem britischen Busunternehmen. Sie ist bemerkenswert gut, und ich habe mich seit meiner Lektüre nie wieder ganz sicher an Bord eines Busses von FirstBus gefühlt, weil ich andere Autoren grundsätzlich als Bedrohung empfinde. Aber Sie, liebe Leserin, lieber Leser, können dieses Buch nicht kaufen. Sie werden nie ein Exemplar besitzen, denn auf der Rückseite ist zu lesen, dass dieses Buch »nicht für den allgemeinen Verkauf« bestimmt sei. Der einzige Grund, dass ich ein Exemplar mein Eigen nennen darf, ist, dass irgendjemand sich seiner – wie es mit so manch edlerer Sache im Leben geschieht – in der Umkleidekabine eines Schwimmbades entledigt hatte, wo ich es eines Nachmittags im April fand.

Und wenn ich es dort nicht auf einer Bank gefunden hätte, hätte ich nie gewusst, dass ich es nicht gefunden hätte.

Derlei glückliche Begebenheiten sind selten. Sie ereignen sich gelegentlich in Gästezimmern oder Gästeklos anderer Leute. Apropos: Wussten Sie, dass es ein Buch gibt, das ausschließlich Fotografien antiker Toiletten in den Cotswolds enthält, einem herrlichen englischen Landstrich? Ich auch nicht, bis ich dort einmal in einem Hotel logierte.

Das Werk von Bohumil Hrabal entdeckte ich unter dem Sofa eines Freundes (ich muss auf dem Boden gelegen haben, das ist so eine Angewohnheit von mir). Es war Hrabals bester Roman, *Ich habe den englischen König bedient* – ich nahm ihn mit, las ihn und war, als ich ihn eine Woche später zurückgab, nicht mehr derselbe. Was das Buch eines anderen Freundes angeht, eines mit französischen Daguerrotypien von Frauen, die sich gegenseitig den Hintern versohlen[2], bin ich unentschieden, ob ich mich darüber freuen soll, es gefunden zu haben. Mein Freund beteuert, es sei ein Geschenk gewe-

2 Serge Nazarieff, *Jeux des Dames Cruelles*, Taschen Verlag, Köln et al. 2000, wenn Sie es genau wissen wollen.

sen, das er aus Höflichkeit nicht ablehnen konnte. Aber meine Freunde sind notorisch unzuverlässig. Er ganz besonders.

All diese Bücher über ländliche Aborte, tschechische Bedienstete und Französinnen mit roten Hintern waren zufällige Begegnungen mit Mr Rumsfeld oder, um genauer zu sein, mit dem unbekannten Unbekannten. Ich hätte nicht gewusst, wie ich nach ihnen suchen sollte. Hätte ich an meinem Computer gesessen, ich hätte keine Ahnung gehabt, dass ich nach ihnen suchen könnte. Ich musste mein Zimmer verlassen. Ich musste dem Zufall eine Chance geben.

Computer sind Maschinen. Das Internet ist letztlich nichts anderes als eine riesige Armee aus Maschinen. Und Maschinen lassen dem Zufall keine Chance. Sie tun genau das, was man ihnen sagt. Deshalb wird man im Internet nichts anderes bekommen als das, wovon man *schon wusste*, dass man es wollte.

Und doch sind solche Begegnungen im norma-
len Leben eher selten, und wir können schlecht
den ganzen Tag damit zubringen, unter Sofas zu
schauen. Darum und deswegen gibt es Die gute
Buchhandlung. Nicht das Kaufhaus und nicht das
Internet, sondern Die gute Buchhandlung. Es handelt sich dabei um einen Verkaufsraum (oder auch
mehrere), wo das unbekannte Unbekannte dieser
Welt auf Tischen ausliegt oder in Regale einsortiert
ist. Es ist ein Ort, an dem Sie alles finden können,
wovon Sie nie wussten, dass Sie es wollten, wo Ihre
Begehrlichkeiten sich unendlich vervielfältigen
können. Nicht befriedigt werden, wohlgemerkt,
denn was wäre der Witz daran, ein Begehren zu be-
friedigen, das Sie schon haben? Davon hätten Sie
nichts. Ein befriedigtes Begehren ist eine traurige
Angelegenheit. Ein neues Begehren dagegen!

Ich habe mich nie besonders für Science-Fiction
erwärmen können. Ich weiß auch nicht, warum.
Es hat mich nie groß interessiert. Ich mag Science
und ich mag Fiction. Aber eben getrennt voneinander. Deshalb weiß ich auch nicht, warum ich eines
Tages einen Roman von Philip K. Dick in die Hand

nahm. Die einzige Erklärung dafür ist, dass er auf einem Tisch in der Buchhandlung lag. Mir gefiel die erste Seite. Mir gefiel die zweite Seite. Und als ich auf Seite zehn angekommen war, wurde mir klar, dass ich das Buch unbedingt kaufen musste. Nachdem ich es ausgelesen hatte, wollte ich mehr. Dringend. Zum Glück schrieb Dick ungefähr so schnell, wie ich lese: 44 Romane und 14 Bände mit Kurzgeschichten. Und noch heute, Jahre später, pflüge ich mich glücklich durch diese Bücher hindurch.

Ich hatte auch niemals das Bedürfnis, ukrainische Kriminalkomödien zu lesen, bis ich eines Tages durch eine Buchhandlung spazierte und mir ein Buch mit dem Titel *Picknick auf dem Eis*[3] in die Hände fiel. Es lag auf einem Tisch – nicht auf dem vorderen, wo die Fußballer-Memoiren liegen, sondern auf dem etwas weiter hinten, wo sich immer die guten Sachen verstecken. Mir gefiel der Titel, mir gefiel der Umschlag – ein Mann mit einer Schusswaffe und einem Pinguin in der Badewanne sitzend –, aber erst als ich das Buch in die Hand

3 Andrej Kurkow, *Picknick auf dem Eis*, übers. von Christa Vogel, Diogenes, Zürich 2000.

genommen, den ersten Absatz gelesen und mich zum Kauf entschlossen hatte, bemerkte ich, dass es vom Autor signiert war. Es gibt Momente, da kann man sein Geld gar nicht schnell genug loswerden. Da will man dem Mädchen an der Kasse nur seinen Zehneuroschein hinwerfen, aus dem Laden rennen und sich ein ruhiges Plätzchen zum Lesen suchen.

Wenn es etwas gibt, das ich in den langen Stunden in guten Buchhandlungen gelernt habe, dann ist es, dass man ein Buch *durchaus* nach seinem Äußeren beurteilen kann. Ich habe *Der Simulant* von Chuck Palahniuk nur deshalb gekauft, weil auf dem Umschlag ein Foto von appetitlich goldglänzenden Fritten prangte und ich einen Riesenhunger hatte. Eine Woche später kaufte ich alle seine anderen Bücher.

Es gibt übrigens etwas, das E-Books für Die gute Buchhandlung geleistet haben: Dank ihrer sind Bücher wieder schön geworden. Noch vor ein paar Jahren waren viele Umschläge eine ziemlich dürftige Angelegenheit: Autor und Titel irgendwie auf ein Agenturfoto von irgendetwas vage Bedeutungsvollem gedruckt. Wenn man es lesen wollte, musste man sich damit arrangieren. Aber plötzlich, nachdem die Margen für gedruckte Bücher[4] etwas höher sind als die für ihre elektrische Alternative, gibt es wieder exquisit gebundene und gestaltete Bücher. Buchhandlungen sind seit mindestens einem Jahrhundert nicht mehr so ansprechend gewesen wie heute.

Bibliomantik: Die Zukunft der Bücher

Ein weiterer Vorteil des gedruckten Buches besteht darin, dass man es durchblättern kann. Es ist leicht, sich einen Eindruck vom Anfang, von der Mitte und vom Ende zu verschaffen. So, wie man das Buch zufällig gefunden hat, kann man zufällig eine Seite, einen Abschnitt oder einen Satz darin finden.

Es ist immer wieder ein merkwürdiges Gefühl, wenn man auf diese Weise auf einen bestimmten Satz stößt. Es ist, als würde er dadurch mit einer

---

4 Die Fachbegriffe lauten ›gedruckte‹ und ›elektronische‹ Bücher, aber mir wäre es sehr viel lieber, man würde von ›physischen‹ und ›metaphysischen‹ Büchern sprechen. Bisher hat meine Kampagne allerdings noch nicht allzu viel Erfolg gehabt.

besonderen Bedeutung aufgeladen. Das ist natürlich völlig irrational, aber so sind wir Menschen eben. Selbst der dickfelligste, durch nichts zu erschütternde Kerl wird erblassen, wenn er an einer beliebigen Stelle ein Buch aufschlägt und die Worte liest: »Schicke dich an, deinem Tod zu begegnen.«

Dieses Gefühl ist so tief in der menschlichen Natur verwurzelt, dass in vielen Kulturen die sogenannte Bibliomantik praktiziert wird, ein Verfahren, um anhand von Büchern in die Zukunft zu blicken. Wenn ein alter Grieche wissen wollte, was ihm bevorstand, schnappte er sich ein Exemplar der *Ilias* und schlug es willkürlich auf irgendeiner Seite auf. Dann deutete er blind auf eine Zeile, las sie und wusste, was das Schicksal für ihn bereithielt. Das waren die *sortes Homericae*.

Die Römer taten nichts anderes mit Vergil und nannten es die *sortes Virgilianae*. Im Mittelalter nahm man die Bibel zu Hilfe, dort hieß das Ganze *sortes Sanctorum*. Es gibt eine Geschichte von Franz von Assisi, der gerade beschlossen hatte, sich von all seinen Besitztümern zu trennen, als er sich plötzlich fragte, ob das auch für seine Bücher gelten sollte, die er sehr liebte. Also schlug er die Bibel auf und fand diese Zeilen:

»Euch ist das Geheimnis des Reiches Gottes gegeben; denen aber draußen widerfährt es alles
durch Gleichnisse.«

Aus irgendeinem Grund schloss er daraus, dass ihm
auch keine Bücher erlaubt seien und dass er sie
ohnehin nicht brauche. Hierüber sind der heilige
Franziskus und ich verschiedener Meinung.

Die katholische Kirche verurteilte später die Bibliomantik als Aberglaube. Aber solange man ein
Bücherregal hat, braucht einen das nicht zu küm-
mern. Als sich der viktorianische Dichter Robert
Browning mit Elizabeth Barrett verlobte, bediente
er sich der Bibliomantik, um zu ergründen, ob der
Verbindung Glück beschieden sein würde. Er trat
also an seinen Bücherschrank und zog ein Buch
heraus, ohne darauf zu achten, worum es sich handelte. Er erhoffte sich davon natürlich eine Bestär-
kung, eine Versicherung aus der mystischen Welt
der Bücher, dass die Liebe stärker sei als alles andere und so weiter.

Kein Wunder, dass er sich ärgerte, als er entdeckte, ein Lehrbuch der italienischen Grammatik
erwischt zu haben. Deshalb tat er das Naheliegende
und senkte seine Ansprüche: Er beschloss, dass es

schon ein gutes Omen wäre, wenn er nur eine Konjunktion fände oder auch ein Possessivpronomen.

Also schlug er das Buch auf, das unter anderem diverse Übersetzungsübungen enthielt. Die erste Zeile, die er las, war diese:

»Wenn wir in der anderen Welt so lieben wie in dieser, werde ich Dich bis in alle Ewigkeit lieben.«

So etwas geht nicht mit einem E-Book.

Ich selbst praktiziere die Bibliomantik übrigens noch immer, und zwar bevorzugt mit Hilfe von P. G. Wodehouse, der die Untiefen meiner Seelenlandschaft in- und auswendig zu kennen scheint. Gerade eben habe ich es wieder einmal versucht, nur um diese Zeile zu finden: »Ich bin ein langweiliger, gedankenloser Tropf.«[5]

Es fällt mir nicht leicht, das zuzugeben, aber die Bibliomantik funktioniert tatsächlich.

5 P. G. Wodehouse, *Jeeves ist eine Klasse für sich*, übers. von Fred Schmitz, Deutscher Taschenbuch Verlag, München 1992, S. 39.

Die Bibliomantik funktioniert bzw. scheint zu funktionieren, weil wir nicht anders können als zu glauben, beim Zufall habe Gott seine Hand im Spiel. Dieser Moment der Entdeckung irgendwo hinten in der Buchhandlung, wenn Sie ein merkwürdiges Bändchen mit einem merkwürdigen Umschlag herausziehen und beschließen: Ja, das werde ich als Nächstes lesen.

Es spielt keine Rolle, um welches Buch es sich handelt. Es ist jenes, das Ihnen ins Auge gesprungen ist. Oder in die Hände gefallen. In einer guten Buchhandlung ist das ein hinreichend guter Grund. In einer guten Buchhandlung sind alle Bücher gut.

Die Kunst des Buchhändlers oder der Buchhändlerin besteht darin zu entscheiden, welche Bücher er oder sie *nicht* ins Sortiment aufnehmen möchte. Es reicht nicht aus, gute Bücher anzubieten, man darf keine schlechten haben.

Hätte eine Buchhandlung sämtliche Bücher im Angebot, wie groß wäre die Chance, das *eine* Buch zu finden, das Sie brauchen? Eine solche Buchhandlung wäre perfekt, wenn Sie bereits *wüssten*, was Sie brauchten, aber das ist, wie gesagt, nicht das, worauf es bei einer Buchhandlung ankommt. Das ist etwas fürs Internet. Nein, die perfekte Buchhandlung ist bescheiden und wählerisch.

Sie sollte es Ihnen ermöglichen, mit verbundenen Augen einzutreten, irgendein Buch in die Hand zu nehmen und dabei etwas Wunderbares zu entdecken. Bitte missverstehen Sie mich nicht: Ich empfehle Ihnen nicht, mit verbundenen Augen Buchhandlungen zu betreten und das auszuprobieren. Wahrscheinlich würden Sie irgendetwas umschmeißen. Oder aus Versehen der Buchhändlerin ins Gesicht fassen. Aber verstehen Sie das Prinzip? Bescheiden und gut bestückt. Ich habe einst besonders gerne Bücher an einem Straßenstand gekauft, der vielleicht sieben Kisten mit Büchern im Angebot hatte. Ich wünschte, ich hätte jedes Einzelne davon lesen können. Leider gibt es diesen Stand nicht mehr.

Der ideale, der absolut perfekte Besuch einer Buchhandlung, den es niemals geben wird, sähe für mich so aus: Ich befinde mich in einer Stadt, in der ich nie zuvor gewesen bin. Am Ende einer kleinen, engen Straße stoße ich auf eine Buchhandlung. Als ich sie betrete, gibt es dort nur ein einziges Buch. Nur eins. Es liegt ohne Schutzumschlag auf einem

Tisch. Ich kann seinen Titel nicht lesen. Ich kaufe es, und es verrät mir alle Geheimnisse des Universums.

Ich weiß natürlich, dass das nie geschehen wird, aber es wäre ein gutes erstes Kapitel für einen Roman.

Die romantische Buchhandlung

Romantik ist, nicht das zu bekommen, was Sie wollten. Jede gute romantische Geschichte lebt davon, dass sich zwei Liebende zu Beginn nicht für einander interessieren. Am Anfang von Jane Austens Roman *Stolz und Vorurteil*[6] kann Elizabeth Bennet Mr Darcy nicht ausstehen. Und Mr Darcy verachtet Elizabeth Bennet. Sie findet ihn unhöflich, arrogant und wortkarg. Er wiederum »hatte ihr anfangs kaum zugestehen wollen, dass sie hübsch sei«, und meinte, ihr fehlten »die Umgangsformen der gebildeten Welt«. Erst später wird ihm klar,

---

6 Hier zitiert in der Neuübersetzung von Manfred Allié und Gabriele Kempf-Allié, S. Fischer Verlag, Frankfurt am Main 2014.

»was für eine Freude doch ein hübsches Augenpaar im Antlitz einer schönen Frau ist«. Und erst sehr viel später, nachdem Elizabeth *zufällig* entdeckt hat, was für ein teures Heim Mr Darcy sein Eigen nennt, vermag auch Elizabeth, ihn zu lieben.

Bei Romeo und Julia ist es genauso. Zu Beginn liebt Romeo ein Mädchen namens Rosalinde und will nur mit ihr und keiner anderen zusammen sein. Julia liebt erst einmal niemanden, ist sich aber ganz sicher, dass sie die Familie Montague hasst. Erst als sich die beiden *zufällig* auf einem Ball begegnen, wird Romeo klar, was für ein Fehlgriff Rosalinde war. Und Julia ruft aus:

»So ein'ge Lieb' aus großem Haß entbrannt!
Ich sah zu früh, den ich zu spät erkannt.«

Natürlich endet das Ganze mit Gifttod und Tränen, aber wenn das nicht höllisch romantisch ist, was dann?

Benedikt und Beatrice aus *Viel Lärm um nichts*, Henry Higgins und Eliza Doolittle aus *My Fair Lady*, Rick und Ilsa aus *Casablanca* – wenn man sie alle gefragt hätte, was sie vom Leben erwarteten, hätte die Antwort gelautet: »Jede(n) andere(n), nur nicht diese(n)«: Das ist die Formel einer jeden romantischen Geschichte. Man hat es nicht beabsichtigt, aber von allen Kneipen in allen Städten dieser Welt gerät man *zufällig* in diese eine, und das Schicksal nimmt seinen Lauf.

Oder, um beim Thema dieses Essays zu bleiben, von allen Buchhandlungen in allen Städten dieser Welt sind Sie *zufällig* in diese eine geraten und haben sich *zufällig* in dieses eine Buch verliebt.

Noch einmal: Das Internet hat es uns unverschämt leicht gemacht, genau das zu kriegen, was wir wollen. Die Partnersuche per Internet erlaubt es uns, die genauen Anforderungen an den Mann oder die Frau zu spezifizieren, die wir erobern wollen. Größe, Gewicht, Einkommen, Sternzeichen, Schuhgröße, Blutgruppe, Allergien, Lieblings-Horrorfilm, Schrittlänge, politische Ansichten und bevorzugtes Frühstücksmüsli – Sie können es sich aussuchen. Sie können die Parameter festlegen. Und wenn Sie das tun, werden Sie genau das bekommen, *wovon Sie bereits wussten, dass Sie es wollten.*

Mr Darcy kriegen Sie so nicht. Und auch nicht Miss Bennet. Romeo hätte »Keine Capulets« eingegeben und Julia »Keine Montagues«. In allem anderen hätten Romeo und Julia durchaus zusammenkommen können. Beide entstammen adligen Familien, sie sind sich ebenbürtig. Sie ist dreizehn, er so um die sechzehn. Ein Algorithmus hätte sie vielleicht zusammengebracht. Aber das eine, was die Beziehung romantisch macht, wäre mit Hilfe der Maschine, des Computers nicht passiert.

Eine moderne Fassung von *Romeo und Julia* würde so aussehen: Er hasst die Capulets. Sie hasst die Montagues. Und so surfen sie ein wenig auf der Seite www.knappvolljährigesinglesinverona.it und kommen einigermaßen zufrieden, aber nicht glücklich mit jemandem zusammen, der ihren Ansprüchen genügt, diese aber nicht verändert.

Stolz und Vorurteil würde sich im Zeitalter des Internet so lesen:

»Es ist eine allgemein anerkannte Tatsache, dass ein alleinstehender Mann im Besitz eines gewissen Vermögens seine Daten und Erwartungen gepostet und sich durch die Antworten gearbeitet haben muss. Leser, ich habe ihn gegoogelt. ENDE«

Natürlich haben die Darcys, die Benedikts und Beatrices das bekommen, was sie wollten – aber sie bekamen das, wovon sie gar nicht wussten, dass sie es wollten. Und das macht ihre Geschichten so romantisch.

Herr, erlöse uns von dem, wovon wir schon wussten, dass wir es wollten. Gib uns neue Bedürfnisse, je ungewöhnlicher, umso besser.

Theologie

In der Philosophie und Theologie existiert die interessante und etwas paradoxe Idee, dass wir Sklaven unserer Bedürfnisse seien. Ihr zufolge sind Bedürfnisse etwas Eigenständiges, von uns Losgelöstes, das uns beherrscht. Hunger zwingt mich, etwas zu essen, Durst zwingt mich, etwas zu trinken (das ist jedenfalls meine Ausrede), und die Neugier zwingt mich, eine Katze zu töten.

Wenn es tatsächlich so sein sollte, werde ich niemals meinen Frieden finden, weil ich mein ganzes Leben damit zubringen werde, diesen ungenügsamen Gebietern genügen zu wollen. Deshalb will der Buddhismus, dass man sich von seinen Bedürfnissen befreit. Deshalb meinte der heilige Augustinus, dass Gott zu dienen die vollkommene Freiheit sei. Meine Ziele als religiöser Visionär fallen deutlich bescheidener aus.

Ich glaube nicht, dass ich ein Sklave meiner Bedürfnisse bin, schon deshalb, weil ich gar nicht wüsste, wie ich die Zeit herumkriegen sollte, wenn ich keine Bedürfnisse hätte. Nähme man mir meinen Durst, hätte ich fünfzehn Stunden am Tag nichts zu tun. Ich bin allerdings gelegentlich *gefangen* in meinen Bedürfnissen. Weil ich weiß, was ich mag, probiere ich nichts Neues aus. Ich habe eine feste Strecke für meinen Morgenspaziergang, ich habe meine Lieblingskneipe, ich habe mein Lieblingsrestaurant. Ich besitze wer weiß wie viele Stunden meiner Lieblingsmusik, die ich mir anhören kann. Ich habe meinen Lieblingswhisky, den ich vor dem Schlafengehen trinke. Und ich habe mir mein Leben so arrangiert, dass ich all das in greifbarer Nähe habe. Vor allem den Whisky.

Deshalb probiere ich nie etwas anderes aus. Um Ihnen ein rührendes kleines Beispiel zu nennen: Vergangenen Montag ist mir klargeworden, dass ich noch nie in meinem Leben Dubonnet getrunken habe. Und es wohl auch nie tun werde. Weil ich der Whisky-Typ bin. Scotch, am liebsten Islay.

Aber ... vielleicht würde ich ja Dubonnet mögen. Man weiß es nicht. Vergangenen Montag ist mir klargeworden, dass ich ihn nie probiert habe. Heute ist Samstag. Genau 236 Meter von meinem Schreibtisch entfernt gibt es einen Laden, der Dubonnet verkauft. Ich bin diese Woche schon mehrmals dort gewesen. Aber ... ich bin gefangen in meinen Bedürfnissen. Ich bevorzuge das bekannte Bekannte. Ich ziehe es vor, die Dinge zu bekommen, von denen ich schon wusste, dass ich sie wollte.

Scheiß drauf. Ich kaufe mir jetzt eine Flasche Dubonnet. Und ich schlage vor, Sie tun dasselbe. Wenn ich zurückkomme, sprechen wir über Geographie.

Geographie

»Als ich ein kleiner Junge war, da waren Landkarten meine große Leidenschaft. Stundenlang konnte ich Südamerika betrachten oder Afrika oder Australien und mir die wunderbarsten Entdeckerreisen ausmalen. Zu jener Zeit gab es auf der Erde noch viele weiße Flecken, und wenn ich auf der Karte einen erblickte, der besonders einladend aussah (was sie ja eigentlich alle tun), zeigte ich mit dem Finger darauf und sagte: Wenn ich groß bin, gehe ich dorthin. Einer dieser Flecken war der Nordpol, das weiß ich noch. Nun, dort bin ich nicht gewesen, und jetzt werde ich es auch nicht mehr versuchen. Der Reiz ist verflogen. Andere lagen um den Äquator und über alle Breiten beider Hemisphären verstreut. An einigen dieser Orte bin ich tatsächlich gewesen und … na, reden wir nicht davon. Aber einen gab es noch immer – den größten und weißesten sozusagen –, der mich besonders reizte.

Zugegeben, inzwischen war er kein weißer Fleck mehr. Seit meinen Kindertagen hatte man ihn mit Flüssen und Seen und Namen versehen. Er war nicht mehr der Ort, für den sich die schönsten Geheimnisse ausmalen ließen – kein heller Fleck mehr, von dem ein Junge träumen konnte.«

Joseph Conrad, *Herz der Finsternis*[7]

---

7 Joseph Conrad, *Jugend. Herz der Finsternis. Das Ende vom Lied*, übers. von Manfred Allié, S. Fischer Verlag, Frankfurt am Main 2009, S. 66.

Heutzutage könnte er Google Earth benutzen. Das bekannte Unbekannte, die weißen Flecken auf Joseph Conrads Landkarte, sie sind inzwischen alle ausgefüllt. Praktisch der letzte Ort, wohin man noch reisen konnte, war der Norden Kanadas. Nach dem Zweiten Weltkrieg waren viele Flugzeuge übrig, es gab jede Menge erfahrene Piloten, sie brummten über die Tundra, machten sich Notizen, machten Fotos und so dem Abenteuer des Entdeckens endgültig den Garaus. Das war der Punkt, an dem wir begannen, uns für andere Planeten zu interessieren. Sie waren alles, was uns blieb.

Es gibt nicht mehr viel bekanntes Unbekanntes. Ein paar Dinge sind natürlich übriggeblieben: die Tiefen der Ozeane, die dunkle Materie, die Frage, warum Tiere schlafen. Obwohl ich finde, dass Joseph Conrad sie mit den Worten »schönste Geheimnisse ausmalen« schon beantwortet hat.

Der Reiz ist verflogen. Auf fast jede Frage, die man stellen kann, gibt es eine Antwort. Es bleiben nur die Fragen, von denen Sie nicht wissen, dass Sie sie stellen könnten, und sie tanzen hinter Ihrem Rücken Cancan. Das unbekannte Unbekannte.

Es gibt sie noch, diese Fragen. Sie sind überall.

Julia erwartet Sie auf dem Ball, wenn Sie nur hingehen. Sie wird immer dort auf Sie warten. Und auch das Buch wartet noch immer auf Sie, das perfekte Buch, das Ihnen jede Frage beantworten wird, von der Sie nicht wussten, dass Sie sie stellen könnten. Es liegt da oben im Regal, in der Ecke, gerade so, dass Sie es noch erreichen können. Das unbekannte Unbekannte, das dort, im hinteren Teil der Buchhandlung, auf Sie wartet wie ein unentdeckter Kontinent.

Das war es, was er meinte, der große Weise, der Prophet: Donald Henry Rumsfeld.

»Die Botschaft lautet, dass es kein ›Wissen‹ gibt. Es gibt Dinge, von denen wir wissen, dass wir sie wissen. Es gibt bekanntes Unbekanntes, also Dinge, von denen wir wissen, dass wir sie nicht wissen. Aber es gibt auch unbekanntes Unbekanntes. Es gibt Dinge, von denen wir nicht wissen, dass wir sie nicht wissen.

Wenn wir also unser Bestes tun und alle Informationen zusammentragen, und wenn wir dann sagen, o. k., so schätzen wir die Situation ein, dann ist das lediglich bekanntes Bekanntes und bekanntes Unbekanntes. Und jedes Jahr entdecken wir neues unbekanntes Unbekanntes.

Das klingt wie ein Rätsel. Es ist kein Rätsel. Es ist eine ernste, sehr wichtige Angelegenheit.«

Aus dem Englischen von Peter Sillem

ALAIN DE BOTTON

*Freunde, die ich
in Buchhandlungen fand*

Das Wertvollste, was ich je in Buchhandlungen gefunden habe, sind Freunde. Freunde wie Montaignes *Essais*, wie Roland Barthes' *Die helle Kammer*, wie W. H. Audens *Gesammelte Gedichte* ...

Die Romantik hat uns die wundervolle, verwegene Idee hinterlassen, dass wir die Einsamkeit überwinden können, wenn wir nur glücklich und entschlossen genug sind, dem einen edlen Wesen zu begegnen, das unser Seelenverwandter ist, jemandem, der alles versteht, was an uns dunkel und seltsam ist, der uns vollkommen erkennt und von uns in unserer Gesamtheit verzaubert ist. Und doch ist das Erbe der Romantik eine Epidemie der Einsamkeit, da wir immer wieder auf die Wahrheit gestoßen werden: die fundamentale Unfähigkeit anderer Menschen, ganz zu erfassen, wer wir wirklich sind.

Es bleibt uns allerdings, neben den Verheißungen der Liebe, eine andere – verlässlichere – Ressource, mit der wir unserer Einsamkeit begegnen können: Bücher.

Henri Matisse, Femme lecture avec les pêches, 1923

Henri Matisse fing mit Anfang zwanzig an, lesende Menschen zu malen, und behielt dies sein Leben lang bei; mindestens dreißig seiner Gemälde widmen sich diesem Thema. Die Bilder verdanken ihre schmerzliche Intensität der Tatsache, dass wir sie als Dokumente der Einsamkeit wahrnehmen, die zumindest zu einem gewissen Grad durch Kultur gelindert wurde. Die Figuren mögen allein sein, ihr Blick ist häufig distanziert und melancholisch, aber griffbereit haben sie den vielleicht besten Ersatzstoff für den Fall, dass unsere unmittelbare Gemeinde uns hängen lässt: Bücher.

Der englische Psychoanalytiker Donald Winnicott – der Mitte des 20. Jahrhunderts praktizierte – war fasziniert davon, wie manche Kinder mit der Abwesenheit ihrer Eltern zurechtkamen. Er machte die Verwendung gewisser »Übergangsobjekte« aus, die die Erinnerung an die elterliche Liebe wach hielten, wenn die Eltern nicht da waren. Ein Teddybär oder eine Schmusedecke konnte ein Instrument sein, das die Erinnerung an das Umsorgtwerden aktivierte, ein Instrument, das in der Regel beweglich, tragbar und immer verfügbar war, wenn die Eltern fehlten.

Winnicott stellte die These auf, dass Kunstwerke für Erwachsene wie komplexere Versionen solcher Art Übergangsobjekte fungieren können. Im Grunde suchen wir in einer Freundschaft nicht unbedingt jemanden, den wir berühren und vor uns sehen können, sondern einen Menschen, der unser Empfinden und unsere Werte teilt und uns diese weiterentwickeln hilft, jemanden, an den wir uns wenden und bei dem wir nach Anzeichen suchen können, dass er empfindet, was wir empfinden, dass er sich von ähnlichen Dingen angezogen, unterhalten oder abgestoßen fühlt. Und eigentümlicherweise scheinen sich gewisse imaginäre Freunde aus der Literatur realer und somit präsenter anzufühlen als unsere Bekanntschaften im echten Leben, selbst wenn Erstere schon seit Jahrhunderten tot sind und auf einem anderen Kontinent lebten. Wir können uns glücklich schätzen, sie zu unseren besten Freunden zu zählen.

Die Literatur ist ein wunderbares Instrument, mittels dessen eine fremde Person das tun kann, was wir als Lügen bezeichnen – und das im Rahmen einer Freundschaft. Und wenn wir solche Kunst-Freunde finden, vertreiben wir die Erfahrung der Einsamkeit. In der Distanz finden wir Intimität. Die Künste erlauben uns, Seelenverwandte von Leuten zu werden, die uns – obwohl sie 1630 oder 1808 geboren wurden – auf eingeschränkte, aber entscheidende Weise echte Gefährten sind. Die Freundschaft mag sogar tiefer gehen als im echten Leben, weil ihr die üblichen Kompromisse, die soziale Interaktionen mit sich bringen, erspart bleiben. Unsere kulturellen Freunde können natürlich keine Konversation machen, und wir können ihnen nicht antworten (außer in unserer Phantasie). Aber sie erreichen, zumindest in einigen wesentlichen Aspekten, den seelischen Raum, in dem wir am verletzlichsten und privatesten sind. Sie mögen unsere neuesten Technologien nicht kennen, sie mögen keine Vorstellung von unseren Familien oder Berufen haben, doch sie verstehen uns – in Bereichen, die uns wirklich wichtig sind – in einem Ausmaß, das zugleich ein bisschen schockierend und höchst aufregend ist.

Angesichts der vielen Unzulänglichkeiten unserer Gemeinschaften im echten Leben gibt uns die Literatur die Möglichkeit, unseren eigenen Stamm zusammenzustellen, Mitglieder über Zeit und Raum hinweg zu gewinnen und lebendige Freunde mit toten Autoren, Architekten, Musikern und Komponisten, Malern und Dichtern zu mischen.

Im 15. Jahrhundert übte die Bibelgeschichte von Tobias und dem Engel eine starke Anziehungskraft auf den italienischen Maler Verrocchio aus – der unter anderem Leonardo da Vinci zu seinen Schülern zählte. Sie handelt von einem jungen Mann, Tobias, der eine lange, gefährliche Reise antreten muss. Doch er hat zwei Gefährten: einen kleinen Hund und einen Engel, der an seiner Seite geht, ihn berät, ermutigt und beschützt.

Der alten religiösen Vorstellung zufolge sind wir niemals vollkommen allein; wir sind immer von besonderen Wesen umgeben, die wir um Hilfe an-

Andrea del Verrocchio, Tobias und der Engel

rufen können. Verrocchios Gemälde ist berührend nicht etwa, weil es eine echte, verlässliche Lösung zeigt, sondern weil es auf die Art von Gemeinschaft verweist, die wir so gern hätten, die uns aber normalerweise so unerreichbar scheint.

Doch es gibt eine verfügbare Version. Natürlich nicht in Form geflügelter Kreaturen mit goldenem Heiligenschein. Sondern in Form der imaginären Freunde, die wir aus der Literatur heranziehen können. Man fühlt sich vielleicht physisch isoliert – im Auto, wartend am Flughafen, auf dem Weg zu einer schwierigen Besprechung, wieder einmal allein beim Abendessen oder während einer Beziehungskrise –, aber in psychologischer Hinsicht ist man nicht allein; Schlüsselfiguren des eigenen imaginären Stamms (die moderne Version von Engeln und Heiligen) sind da: ihre Perspektive, ihre Denkweisen, ihre Sicht der Dinge sind in deinem Kopf, so als säßen sie wirklich neben dir und würden dir ins Ohr flüstern. Und so können wir den schwierigen Phasen unserer Existenz nicht nur mit unseren eigenen begrenzten Ressourcen entgegentreten, sondern begleitet von der geballten Weisheit der gütigsten, intelligentesten Stimmen der Vergangenheit.

In Anbetracht der gewaltigen Rolle, die die Traurigkeit in unseren Leben spielt, ist dies eine der herausragenden emotionalen Kompetenzen: zu wissen, wie man sich mit den kulturellen Werken umgibt, die am besten geeignet sind, unsere Panik oder unseren Verfolgungswahn in Trost und Nahrung umzumünzen.

Aus dem Englischen von Britt Somann-Jung

MARION BRASCH

Wie ich in New Jersey nach Paterson
suchte und ihn in Kanada fand

Das ist eine Szene aus dem Film *Paterson* von Jim Jarmusch. Der schüchterne und wortkarge Busfahrer und Poet Paterson aus Paterson/New Jersey liest seiner Freundin gerade ein Gedicht seines Lieblingsdichters William Carlos Williams vor, der der Stadt ein ganzes Gedichtepos gewidmet hat.

Paterson ist einer meiner absoluten Lieblingsfilme, und als ich vor einem Jahr in Amerika war, wollte ich unbedingt in diese Stadt. Ein Freund sagte, Paterson sei nicht so interessant, ich solle lieber zum Hillside Cemetery in Lyndhurst/New Jersey fahren, wo William Carlos Williams begraben sei, dort liege ja auch Joey Ramone und außerdem habe man einen tollen Blick auf Manhattan. Also bestieg ich den Bus Richtung Paterson.

Auf halber Strecke stieg ich aus, fand den Friedhof, auch die Gräber von Joey Ramone und William Carlos Williams.

Und auch den Blick auf Manhattan fand ich gut.

Danach fuhr ich zurück, und weil ich William Carlos Williams jetzt gewissermaßen persönlich kannte, machte ich mich auf die Suche nach dem Gedichtband, den Paterson in Jarmuschs Film in den Händen hält.

Diese Ausgabe konnte ich nirgendwo finden, doch zwei Wochen später entdeckte ich in einer kleinen Buchhandlung in Montréal *Paterson*, jenen Gedichtband, der im Film auch im Bücherregal des Busfahrers lag.

Der Besitzer der Buchhandlung war ein wortkarger Mann, der die gleichen Schuhe trug wie ich.

LAETITIA COLOMBANI

Ich erinnere mich an die allererste Signierstunde in einer Buchhandlung für meinen ersten Roman *Der Zopf*. Mich hatte die Buchhandlung der Kleinstadt bei Bordeaux, in der ich aufgewachsen bin, eingeladen. Zu meiner Überraschung traf ich dort auf einen Lehrer von meiner Grundschule, den ich 30 Jahre lang nicht gesehen hatte (!). Als Kind hatte er mich zum Schreiben animiert, denn er fand, dass ich viel Phantasie hatte. Ich habe ihm jede Woche einen kleinen Text zu egal welchem Thema gegeben, den er dann korrigierte und mit Anmerkungen versah. Am Ende des Jahres sagte er zu meinen Eltern: »Eines Tages wird sie Schriftstellerin.« Da war ich zehn. Und dann kam er also in dieser Buchhandlung mit den Worten auf mich zu: »Siehst du, ich hatte recht. Du hast zwar 30 Jahre dafür gebraucht, aber du hast es geschafft!« Diesen Moment werde ich nie vergessen.

Aus dem Französischen von Isabel Kupski

JENNIFER EGAN

Im Sommer nach meinem dritten Collegejahr – es muss 1984 gewesen sein – jobbte ich in New York und wohnte mit meiner besten Freundin zur Untermiete in einem Apartment an der Houston Street. Damals gab es in New York noch viele unabhängige Buchhandlungen, und bei einem Spaziergang im West Village (ein Viertel, in dem ich mich 35 Jahre später immer noch verlaufen kann) stieß ich auf eine kleine Buchhandlung, die ich noch nie gesehen hatte und die ich auch nie wiederfinden sollte. Der Eigentümer empfahl mir James Salters *Ein Spiel und ein Zeitvertreib*. Ich hatte noch nie von Salter gehört, und die schillernde Sinnlichkeit seines Schreibens verblüffte mich. Noch heute finde ich kaum einen Roman so sexy wie *Ein Spiel und ein Zeitvertreib*, und ich habe sogar schon darauf zurückgegriffen, bevor ich mich an Sexszenen für meine eigenen Romane gemacht habe!

Aus dem Englischen von Britt Somann-Jung

ORKUN ERTENER

Der Terrorist

Die Buchhandlung erstreckte sich über zwei Etagen eines schmalen Fachwerkhauses, in die obere kam man über eine Holztreppe, die in meiner Erinnerung knarrt, doch sicher bin ich mir nicht. Damals jedenfalls hielt ich jeden meiner Schritte für zu laut und jede meiner Bewegungen für zu auffällig. Überall, besonders hier. Es war dunkler als in den anderen Buchläden, es roch anders, älter und schwerer, bildete ich mir ein, es gab andere Bücher. Bücher von Enzensberger, Cardenal, Meinhof und Fried, das Kursbuch, den Freibeuter und den Tintenfisch, Bücher über die Friedensbewegung und die Revolutionäre in Lateinamerika, Bücher über die Befreiung der Frau und den männlichen Orgasmus, Bücher für Kinder und Jugendliche, die das Neinsagen lernen wollen. Alle diese Bücher hätte man auch in den anderen Buchhandlungen der Stadt bekommen, wenn man wusste, wonach man suchte, es gab sie sicher auch in der Stadtbücherei, die so etwas wie mein zweites Zuhause war. Aber hier waren sie sichtbar, hier erfuhr ich, dass es sie gab. Hier sah ich, was ich bisher versäumt hatte und um keinen Preis länger versäumen wollte.

Der Buchhändler führte sein Geschäft allein, glaube ich, an Mitarbeiter kann ich mich nicht erinnern. Er war doppelt so alt wie ich, in meinen Augen damals furchteinflößend alt und erfahren, aus meiner heutigen Warte blutjung und mit einem solchen Geschäft an einem solchen Ort verwegen optimistisch. Er hatte lange Haare, einen Bart und eine runde Brille. Den Strickpulli, den er trug, trug er in meiner Erinnerung auch im Sommer, aber das ist sicher nur ein eingefrorenes Bild. Als mein Vater ihn einmal sah, sagte er, der Mann sehe aus wie ein Terrorist, bestenfalls wie ein Mitglied der aufrührerischen neuen Partei, die kurz zuvor gegründet worden war und noch Jahrzehnte brauchen sollte, um über einen eigenen Kanzlerkandidaten nachdenken zu müssen. Mir gefiel, was mein Vater sagte. Ich war fünfzehn und suchte, was meine Eltern und die meisten meiner Lehrer nie gefunden hatten.

Nachdem ich mich einmal getraut hatte, das Fachwerkhaus zu betreten, wofür ich eine Weile brauchte, kam ich immer wieder. Ich stöberte und blätterte, las Klappentexte und so viele Absätze wie möglich, blieb aber nie lange, weil ich befürchtete, der Buchhändler könne mich für einen Dieb halten. Ich weiß nicht mehr, ob ich in diesen ersten Monaten ein Buch gekauft habe, viel Geld hatte ich nicht, ich weiß auch nicht, ob wir uns grüßten, wenn ich hereinkam, aber ich bin mir sicher, dass wir nie miteinander sprachen. Eines Tages sagte er plötzlich: »Du liest viel, stimmt's?« Ohne eine Antwort abzuwarten, drückte er mir zwei unverkäufliche Leseexemplare in die Hand, einen Lassahn und einen Irving, und wünschte mir viel Vergnügen.

Ich ging mit meinen Büchern nach Hause und kam immer wieder. Einen Großteil meines Geldes gab ich danach hier aus, bis ich die enge Stadt drei, vier Jahre später für immer verließ. Beim Bezahlen glaubte ich immer, in seinen Blicken zu erkennen, was er von meiner Wahl hielt. Der Buchhändler hatte einen Kunden gewonnen und mir dafür etwas gegeben, was ich für immer behalten konnte. Ich war ein Leser, das hatte er gesehen, das konnte ich nun selbst glauben, und an jedem Ort, an dem ich in den Jahrzehnten danach war, wusste ich, wohin ich gehen musste, um etwas zu finden, das mir gefehlt hatte, obwohl ich vorher nicht ahnte, dass es existiert.

HÉLÈNE GESTERN

Zufällig

Von den Dutzenden, wenn nicht Hunderten Büchern, die ich per Zufall entdeckt habe, erinnere ich mich an zwei ganz besonders. Das erste hat mein Leben verändert. Ich war Studentin und ging durch eine vertraute Straße, wie gewöhnlich hielt ich bei den Kisten des Antiquars, der auf dem Gehsteig die Bücher auslegte, die er bei einer Haushaltsauflösung angekauft hatte. Oder war es die Auslage einer heute verschwundenen Buchhandlung eine Straße weiter? Meine Erinnerung lässt mich im Stich, aber ich weiß noch, dass man auf diesem Gehsteig zu einem unschlagbaren Preis alles und nichts fand – vor allem alles. Ich entdeckte ein Buch, bei José Corti erschienen, ein außergewöhnlicher und anspruchsvoller Verleger, einer der letzten in Frankreich, der seine Bände nicht aufschnitt, seine Bücher musste man also immer mit einem Papiermesser in der Hand lesen. Der Titel war großartig, *Archive der Stille*. Die Schönheit der wenigen Seiten, die ich beim flüchtigen Blättern in dem gut erhaltenen Band überflog, machte mich sprachlos. Eine fremdartige Dichtung, explosiv, atemberaubend, die Sprache erschien mir dennoch vertraut. Ich habe den Band gekauft. Ich habe ihn wieder und wieder gelesen, bis ich ihn auswendig konnte. Sogar meine Diplomarbeit und ein Drittel meiner Dissertation habe ich über Jacques Garelli geschrieben, und einmal hatte ich das Glück, ihm persönlich zu begegnen. Mit ihm, durch ihn und dank ihm habe ich das Gefühl, das äußerste Rätsel der Sprache durchdringen, das Ausmaß ihrer Kraft verstehen zu können. Gewissermaßen, auch wenn er es nie wissen wird, gehört dieser Dichter, der in Frankreich vor allem für seine philosophischen Schriften bekannt ist, zu den Schriftstellern, die mich selbst zur Schriftstellerin gemacht haben, wenn ich das so sagen darf.

Das zweite Buch habe ich in einem Pariser Geschäft einer großen französischen Kaufhauskette gefunden. Dort kann man alles kaufen, Bücher, Musik, Telefone, Kopfhörer, Fernseher ... Der Ort ist ein bisschen kalt, man geht nur hin, um zu konsumieren. Mein Partner und ich wollten lediglich einen gewöhnlichen Einkauf machen. Und während wir an der Kasse in der Schlange standen, entdeckte ich ein zur Seite gelegtes Buch. Ein Kunde musste es lustlos oder in Eile dort abgelegt und sich noch vor der Bezahlung verdrückt haben. Es war ein Taschenbuch, eins aus der Folio-Reihe. Es war schön, der Umschlag hat sofort meinen Blick gefangengenommen: die Silhouette einer schmalen, biegsamen Frau, verloren in zartgrüner Natur, ein großer orangefarbener Schirm über ihrem Kopf. Leuchtende, aber zurückhaltende Farben, ein dickes Buch – so wie man es mag, wenn man gerne liest. Seine Schönheit kontrastierte mit der Hässlichkeit der Umgebung. Ich kannte weder den Titel (*Der Duft des Ingwers*) noch den Autor (Oswald Wynd), aber der Gedanke, dieses schöne Buch an der Ladenkasse liegen zu lassen, machte mich ganz traurig. Ich habe es einfach zu meinen Einkäufen gepackt und es sofort gelesen. *Der Duft des Ingwers* wurde von einem in Japan geborenen Schotten geschrieben. Es ist ein historischer Roman, der von einer unmöglichen Verbindung zwischen einer jungen Frau aus der englischen Bourgeoisie und einem Japaner erzählt. Aber misstrauen Sie dieser schnulzigen Zusammenfassung: Die Heldin ist eine wunderbare Figur, und besonders wunderbar ist die Geschichte, ich meine die große Geschichte,

die den Figuren und ihren Schicksalen Kontur ver-
leiht. Dieses Buch hat mich genauso mitgerissen
wie ergriffen. In dieser Zeit habe ich so gut wie
keine Romane gelesen, weil mir entweder die Lust
oder die Zeit fehlte, aber dieser Roman hat sich wie
ein Fanal in meine Erinnerung eingebrannt. Als ich
diesen Roman las, habe ich die ursprüngliche, drän-
gende und ungetrübte Lust wiederentdeckt, eine
Geschichte zu erzählen, dicht wie das Leben.

Aus dem Französischen von Isabel Kupski

VALENTIN GROEBNER

Das Schwierige, das Leichte,
das Finden, das Gefundenwerden

Als ich ein schüchterner und brotloser Nachwuchswissenschaftler war, schwärmte ich für eine Bibliothekarin. Das war naheliegend, Bibliotheken sind ein guter Ort für Nachwuchswissenschaftler, die eigene Ernsthaftigkeit und Schüchternheit zur Schau zu stellen – man kann dort gut arbeiten, und der Eintritt ist umsonst. Die Bibliothekarin hatte eine Brille, und Frauen mit Brille fand ich ohnehin anziehend. Ich erfand Gründe, um sie anzusprechen, und alle hatten mit dem Finden zu tun, dem Finden des richtigen Buches. »Können Sie mir vielleicht sagen, wo ich …?« Ihre Antworten fielen immer sehr sachlich aus, leider, und eher knapp. Dann zog ich um, und in der neuen Stadt gab es auch große Bibliotheken, aber zum ersten Mal eine Lieblingsbuchhandlung. Eine Lieblingsbuchhandlung ist eine, in der auf großen Tischen die Neuerscheinungen aufgestellt sind, die man immer schon lesen wollte; man wusste nur nicht, dass es sie gibt.

Der Besitzer der Buchhandlung war streng. Er

war wortkarg, knurrig und hatte feste Vorstellungen von dem, was das gute Buch war, das richtige gute Buch. Am liebsten hätte er nur solche im Sortiment gehabt; zu den anderen zog er nur stumm und missbilligend die Augenbrauen hoch. Die Buchhandlung lag in einer Seitenstraße in der Nähe der Kunsthochschule, deswegen gab es nicht nur Belletristik, sondern auch Theorie, Fotografie, Architektur und schöne Bildbände. Und es gab eine Buchhändlerin, und ich vergaß die Bibliothekarin. Sie war auch streng, aber hübsch, mit Hornbrille, und viel gesprächiger. Wir verabredeten uns auf einen Kaffee. Leider gab es ein Missverständnis, und wir warteten zur selben Zeit in zwei verschiedenen Cafés aufeinander.

Wenn es am Anfang schwierig ist, bleibt es schwierig. Nach dem ersten Missverständnis kamen noch ein paar andere, und es wurde nichts mit der Buchhändlerin und mir. Aber als ich ein Vierteljahr später wieder in die Buchhandlung kam, strahlte sie mich an und sagte, sie hätte genau das richtige Buch für mich, gerade erschienen. *Aah, das Love-Ding!* hieß es.

Ich schlug es auf, und es war wirklich genau das, was ich gesucht hatte: Witzig, bookish und unsentimental klug über all die endlosen Widersprüche der Objektwahl.

Wenn es am Anfang schwierig ist, bleibt es schwierig. Wenn es am Anfang leicht ist, bleibt es nicht leicht, weder bei Büchern noch bei Liebesobjekten. Aber in Buchhandlungen habe ich gelernt, dass ich normalerweise nicht das finde, wonach ich gesucht habe. Dafür etwas anderes, das mir besser und weiter hilft, nur hatte ich eben vorher nicht gewusst, dass es existiert. Meistens ist es ein Buch. Das Strenge und das Leichte stehen in den Regalen dicht nebeneinander. Das Finden und das Gefundenwerden auch.

YANN MARTEL

Meinen glücklichsten Buchhandelsfund machte ich in Indien. Es war keine konventionelle Buchhandlung; es war nur ein Mann, der auf dem Gehweg saß und Bücher ordentlich auf einer Decke ausgebreitet hatte. Ein Buch-wallah. Ich überflog sein Angebot. Es war die übliche Mischung: aktuelle indische und angloamerikanische Bücher, von anspruchsvoll bis reißerisch, dazwischen vereinzelte Klassiker – und ein französisches Buch. Ich nahm es in die Hand. Wie bist du denn hergekommen, fragte ich mich. Und wie eigentümlich: Es handelte sich um die französische Übersetzung iranischer Kurzgeschichten von 1932. Es hieß *Trois Gouttes de Sang* und war von Sadeq Hedayat. Um es gleich vorwegzunehmen: Ich hatte keine Ahnung von iranischer Literatur. Ich hatte noch nie von Hedayat gehört. Ich fragte den Buch-wallah, wie er an dieses Buch gekommen war. Er blickte kurz hin und schien so ratlos wie ich. Er zuckte mit den Achseln. Also kaufte ich es und war begeistert. Es war das erste Mal, dass ich durch das imaginäre Fenster der Literatur auf den Iran blickte. Jahre später habe ich den Iran bereist. Ich glaube kaum, dass ich das getan hätte, wenn ich nicht vorher auf Hedayat gestoßen wäre.

Aus dem Englischen von Britt Somann-Jung

JÖRG MAURER

Das Märchen vom schwarzen Ritter

Es war einmal ein kleines Königreich, in dem furchtbar viel und gern gelesen wurde. In der schmucken Hauptstadt reihte sich eine Buchhandlung an die andere, und wohin das Auge auch schweifte, überall fanden sich Schmökerstuben, Antiquariate und bestens sortierte Librarien. Es war eine Stadt, die eigentlich nur aus Buchhandlungen bestand. Nein, das stimmt nicht ganz, es gab auch Buchbindereien, Leselampengeschäfte und Berufsfachschulen für Buchhändler. Einmal im Jahr prämierte der König die beste Buchhandlung, wobei er großen Wert auf flauschige Teppiche, gemütliche Sitzecken und kompetente Beratung in allen erdenklichen Genres legte. Und so lebten und lasen alle zufrieden dahin. Doch eines Tages kam ein Fremder in die Stadt. Wortlos betrat er »Toms Leselust«, griff sich das erstbeste Buch und blätterte es durch. Blechern lachte er auf, als er bei der letzten Seite angelangt war, dann zerdrückte er das Buch mit der bloßen Hand. Das zweite ließ er achtlos fallen, das dritte stellte er umgekehrt und zerknittert ins Regal zurück. Der König rief den blondgelockten Hauptmann der Leibgarde zu sich und sprach: »Ich gebe dir meine liebliche und belesene Tochter zur Frau, wenn du herausfindest, was dieser Fremde will. Gebiete dann seinem Treiben Einhalt.« Der blonde Jüngling beobachtete den seltsamen Gast. Der stand nun schon in der dritten Buchhandlung und hatte bisher alle Bücher durchgelesen. »Was treibt Ihr da, edler Herr?«, fragte er den Fremden, doch dieser antwortete nicht. »Missfallen Euch die Geschichten, die Ihr gelesen habt?«, fragte er, doch wieder schwieg der Fremde. Der blonde Jüngling fragte noch ein drittes Mal und legte dem Fremden dabei die Hand auf den Oberarm. Doch wie erschrak er! Eiskalt war die Schulter des Fremden, und ihn fröstelte. »Ich lese nicht«, sagte der Fremde mit abgehackter Stimme. »Ich scanne und digitalisiere. Freut euch, ihr Büchernarren. All die wunderbaren Geschichten sind fürderhin auf einem daumennagelgroßen Chip verfügbar. Ihr braucht die Schwarten nicht mehr mit euch herumzuschleppen, ihr habt sie alle in euren Smartphones gespeichert.« Schon wieder hatte er die letzte Seite eines herrlichen Romans mit Goldschnitt und besticktem Kalbsledereinband fertiggelesen, und er drohte das

Kunstwerk in seiner eisernen Faust zu zermalmen. Da packte der blondgelockte Jüngling den schwarzen Ritter am Bein, um ihn nach draußen zu zerren und ihm dergestalt Einhalt zu gebieten. Doch der war keinen Zoll vom Platz zu bewegen. Der junge Recke griff sich die Bibliotheksleiter aus Ebenholz und nahm Anlauf, um sie dem schwarzen Ungetüm in die Seite zu rammen. Doch der Mann aus Stahl stand wie eingeschraubt. Da erinnerte sich der lockige Gardehauptmann an eine Geschichte, die er einst gelesen hatte. War da nicht ein unbezwingbarer Held zwischen den Schulterblättern verwundbar gewesen? Er näherte sich dem schwarzen Ritter von hinten, und tatsächlich gab es in der Mitte des Rückens einen Kippschalter. Den legte er um, und sofort wich alles Leben aus dem eisernen Ungetüm, und es gab keinen Laut mehr von sich. Der kluge Jüngling erhielt die Tochter des überglücklichen Königs zur Frau. Und noch heute legen dir Buchhändler, wenn sie ein Gespräch mit dir suchen oder dich beraten wollen, die Hand scheinbar freundschaftlich von hinten zwischen die Schulterblätter und führen dich auf diese Weise herum. Sei nicht böse über diese Angewohnheit. Es ist nur sicherheitshalber.

THORSTEN
NAGELSCHMIDT

Im April 2019 befinde ich mich auf einer Lese-
reise an der Ostküste der USA. Sechs von sieben
gemeinsamen Auftritten liegen bereits hinter uns,
als mein Übersetzer Tim und ich im Platzregen ins
Penn Book Center in Philadelphia humpeln. Tags
zuvor sind wir in einen heftigen Autounfall geraten. Auf einer Autobahnbrücke in Delaware hat
uns ein Tanklaster gerammt, mehrmals. Wir haben
uns mehrmals gedreht, aber zum Glück nicht über-
schlagen. Wie durch ein Wunder wurde niemand
schwer verletzt oder getötet.

Mein Gesicht und meine Hände sind zerschnit-
ten und verschorft, Tim zieht ein Bein nach. Ich
finde, dass wir ziemlich cool aussehen. Wie Leute,
die etwas erlebt und mit ziemlicher Sicherheit etwas zu erzählen haben.

Im Kofferraum von Tims Honda Civic, der nun
als Totalschaden auf einem Schrottplatz in Delaware sein Restdasein fristet, ist beim Unfall eine
Kiste Merlot zu Bruch gegangen, der Inhalt wurde
über einen Teil der zum Verkauf bestimmten Exem-

plare meines Romans verteilt. »The ones that smell like alcohol are five dollars extra today«, scherzen wir, als wir die Bücher an der Kasse des Penn Book Center drapieren. Wir scherzen überhaupt recht viel an diesem Tag. Wir stehen wohl noch unter Schock und zelebrieren eine Art Dem-Galgen-noch-einmal-entwischt-Humor, offensiv, heroisch, todesverachtend.

Zu Beginn unserer Reise habe ich mir vorgenommen, an jedem Auftrittsort mindestens ein Buch eines lokalen Autors zu kaufen. Tim erzählt mir von der großen Lyriktradition in Philadelphia, doch alle Bändchen, die ich in die Hand nehme, umgibt schon rein äußerlich eine Aura von heiligem Ernst, Formstrenge und Academy, die mir in meinem gegenwärtigen Zustand als blutleer und schal erscheint. Ich brauche etwas Lebendigeres, etwas Wildes, Hartes. Ich habe seit jeher eine Schwäche für Tough-Guy-Literatur. Man könnte von Guilty Pleasure sprechen, wäre die Idee von Schuld in diesem Kontext nicht so verabscheuenswert.

Plötzlich springt mich aus mehreren Metern Entfernung ein Paperback an. Es thront auf einem der brusthohen Regale in der Belletristikabteilung und zeigt einen Mann in Jeans und Lederjacke, der mit ausgebreiteten Armen am Zaun einer Weide lehnt. Die Hände des Mannes sind schmutzig, und sein Kopf ist gesenkt, das Gesicht verborgen im Schatten eines mächtigen weißen Stetsons. Verbirgt er den Blick mit Absicht vor der Kamera? Lacht oder weint er, oder hat er nur etwas ins Auge bekommen? Der Mann wirkt erschöpft und beschädigt, erledigt aber ist er noch nicht.

Der Titel des Buches ist *Cowboys Are My Weakness*, die Autorin heißt Pam Houston. Ich schlage es auf. Das Buch ist von 1992 und enthält zwölf Kurzgeschichten, in denen es um Schneestürme, Stromschnellen und um harte, schweigsame Männer und Frauen in der nordamerikanischen Wildnis geht. Genau so etwas brauche ich jetzt. Schließlich bin auch ich so eine Art Cowboy, beschädigt und gezeichnet, aber vorerst noch einmal davongekommen.

Pam Houston kommt nicht aus Philadelphia, immerhin aber aus dem knapp 40 Meilen entfernten Trenton, New Jersey, was sie für mich als halbwegs lokale Autorin qualifiziert. Ich kaufe das Buch. Ich habe nicht danach gesucht und keine Ahnung, warum es 27 Jahre nach seinem Erscheinen später derart prominent ausgestellt wurde. Man sollte doch meinen, die wenigen Aufsteller seien den vielen Neuerscheinungen vorbehalten. Doch amerikanische Indiebuchhandlungen funktionieren anders, zumindest bilde ich mir das gerne so ein. Und was die Tough-Guy-Literatur angeht: den Aspekt Guy hielt ich dabei schon immer für mindestens vernachlässigenswert.

LORI NELSON SPIELMAN

SPIELMAN

Was ich in einer
Buchhandlung fand

Es war der 9. November, der Morgen nach der amerikanischen Präsidentschaftswahl 2016. Ich war lange aufgeblieben und hatte mir die Wahlergebnisse angesehen, war dann fassungslos ins Bett gegangen und drei Stunden später zutiefst angewidert aufgewacht. Meine Augen brannten, als ich zu »Schuler«, meiner liebsten unabhängigen Buchhandlung, fuhr.

Die Menschen, die ich aus dem Auto sah, waren mir mit einem Mal suspekt. Nach der Hoffnung und Zuversicht, die mir die vergangenen acht Jahre Auftrieb gegeben hatten, machte sich nun Verzweiflung breit. Ein tiefer Graben schien sich zwischen mir und meinen Mitbürgern aufzutun. Hat die Frau mit dem Handy am Ohr für ihn gestimmt? Und was ist mit den Typen an der Bushaltestelle? Begrüßen sie die hasserfüllte Rhetorik des Präsidenten in spe? Meine ganze Weltanschauung lag in Trümmern.

Ich betrat den Laden; der vertraute Duft nach Büchern und Kaffee tröstete mich für einen Moment. Es war ruhig an diesem Morgen, als wenn auch die Buchhandlung trauerte.

Meine Fingerspitzen streiften die Buchrücken, als ich durch die Gänge wanderte. Ich suchte nach etwas, worin ich mich verlieren konnte, eine Geschichte, durch die ich mich weniger allein fühlte. Ich sehnte mich nach einer Erzählung, die mich aufheiterte und mir Hoffnung machte. Aber an diesem Tag nahm mich nichts gefangen; die leichteren Romane passten nicht zu meiner düsteren Stimmung, und die ernsten Bücher waren zu schwere Kost.

Als ich mich zum Gehen wandte, bemerkte ich Rhoda, die mich von einer Leiter beobachtete. Rhoda, eine kluge, couragierte Frau mit tadellosem Literaturgeschmack, war meine Lieblingsbuchhändlerin. Unsere Blicke trafen sich. In ihren Augen spiegelten sich die gleiche Trauer, Enttäuschung und Verlorenheit, die ich empfand. Sie stieg von ihrer Leiter herunter. Wir sagten nichts. Wir nahmen uns in die Arme, eine kräftige, verbindende, vereinende Umarmung, die mir zeigte, dass ich nicht allein war.

Ich war auf der Suche nach Hoffnung in die Buchhandlung gekommen. Ich fand sie in Rhoda.

Aus dem Englischen von Britt Somann-Jung

PETER PRANGE

B&B: Von Betten und Büchern

Fast immer, wenn ich eine Buchhandlung betrete, muss ich an das Bettengeschäft meiner Eltern denken. Das liegt nicht daran, dass Bücher – wahlweise als Einschlafhilfe oder Begleiter durch schlaflose Nächte – häufig im Bett gelesen werden. Auch die Alliteration ist nicht der Grund, so wenig wie die Tatsache, dass mein Vater in seinem kleinen Büro stets Romane las, wenn keine Kundschaft im Laden war. Der Grund ist vielmehr …

Nun, alles fing damit an, dass ich dem Bettengeschäft meiner Eltern meinen Beruf verdanke. Und das kam so …

Als kleiner Junge wollte ich, wie so ziemlich alle kleinen Jungen, in die Fußstapfen meines Vaters treten, sprich: das Bettengeschäft übernehmen, das bereits mein Großvater gegründet hatte. Doch dann wurde ich Zeuge eines Erwachsenengesprächs, in dem mein Vater und ein paar andere Männer über ihre Berufe sprachen. »Ich mache in Versicherungen«, stellte sich der Erste vor. »Und ich in Draht«, erklärte der Zweite. »Und ich«, sagte mein Vater,

»ich mache in Betten.« Das war mir so peinlich, dass ich auf der Stelle beschloss, DICHTER zu werden.

Von diesem Entschluss bis zu meinem ersten Buch war es natürlich ein weiter Weg. Doch auch das wichtigste Rüstzeug, das ich zur Ausübung meines neu gewählten Berufs brauchte – Menschenkenntnis –, erwarb ich im elterlichen Geschäft. Während meiner Schulzeit begleitete ich meinen Vater täglich bei den Auslieferungen. Diese endeten, wie konnte es anders sein, meist im Schlafzimmer. Und nirgendwo sonst geben Menschen sich so ungehemmt preis wie an diesem zweitprivatesten aller Orte. »Mein Mann schläft ja gern nackt, ich dagegen friere sogar im Sommer. Aber wenn ich mich an meinen Mann kuschele, um mich aufzuwärmen, sagt er immer: ›Geh mir weg mit deine Eisbeine.‹«

Um zu lernen, wie solche Alltagserfahrungen sich verdichten lassen, suchte ich nach Vorbildern. Diese fand ich in der Buchhandlung »Katerlöh«, der führenden, weil einzigen Buchhandlung in meiner kleinen Heimatstadt Altena. Das ganze Trinkgeld, das ich bei den Betten-Auslieferungen einnahm, habe ich in diesem maximal 20 Quadratmeter großen Laden ausgegeben. Und ich habe keinen einzigen Pfennig bereut. Der Grund dafür war die exzellente Beratung, die ich bei Katerlöh erfuhr. Weil ich in meiner Jugend sehr klein war, trug ich, um den oft einen Kopf größeren Mädchen zu imponieren, eine Schlägermütze, die mich in den Augen der Buchhändlerin allerdings zum Intellektuellen stempelte. Darum versorgte sie mich von frühester Jugend an vorzugsweise mit Werken französischer Existentialisten. Von denen mochte ich am liebsten Sartre. Bei dem gab es immer »Stellen«, also wenigstens auf dem Papier solche Erlebnisse, die mir aufgrund meiner unzureichenden Körpergröße im wirklichen Leben versagt blieben.

Und damit schließen sich die Kreise. Beide Branchen, der Buch- wie der Bettenhandel, sind sehr beratungsintensiv, und Erfolg hat nur, wer das Vertrauen des Kunden gewinnt. Ich muss den Kunden kennen und wissen, was ihm gefällt und was er will, und im Idealfall ist dessen Vertrauen so groß, dass er meinem Rat blind folgt. Das gelang meinem Vater mit vielen seiner Kunden, und das gelang der Buchhändlerin von Katerlöh bei mir.

Dabei gibt es aber einen großen Unterschied: Im

Bettenhandel ist die Warenvielfalt viel geringer und die Abfolge der Novitäten wesentlich langsamer als im Buchgeschäft. Wenn ich als Bettenhändler die Vorzüge meiner Matratzen und Bettdecken kenne, die sich oft jahrelang unverändert im Markt behaupten, kann ich schon kompetent beraten. Von einem Buchhändler aber wird erwartet, dass er den Kunden durch ein Labyrinth von jährlich hunderttausend Neuerscheinungen führt – bei einer viel größeren Zahl von Kunden mit individuell unendlich ausdifferenzierten Vorlieben und Neigungen.

Trotzdem passiert dieses kleine, große Wunder Tag für Tag, Stunde für Stunde, in rund 4000 Buchhandlungen in Deutschland. Davor kann ich mich nur verbeugen und sage – als Autor auch ganz egoistisch – DANKE!

DANIEL SPECK

Espace Diwan

Ein rostiger Benzinkanister. Ich stehe in einem Antiquitätenladen in der Medina von Tunis, und der Händler nennt mir seinen Preis. Nach einer Woche Recherche ist dieser Rommelschrott das einzige Relikt des Afrikakorps, das ich aufgestöbert habe. Ansonsten ist die Erinnerung an die deutsche Besatzung bei den Menschen verblasst; viele wissen nicht mehr, dass die Wehrmacht einst wie die Heuschrecken eingefallen war, um bald darauf von den Alliierten vertrieben zu werden.

Ich bin auf Recherche für meinen Roman *Piccola Sicilia*, der von einem deutschen Soldaten erzählt, der in Nordafrika einem italienischen Juden das Leben rettet. In Tunis will ich die Schauplätze finden und mit den Menschen sprechen. Eigentlich aber komme ich zu spät, die Welt von damals existiert nicht mehr. Die Italiener emigrierten nach dem Krieg, und nach dem Sechstagekrieg haben auch die meisten Juden das Land verlassen. Ich konnte keinen Zeitzeugen finden.

Manchmal überkommt mich bei der Recherche

ein Gefühl der Trauer über eine verlorene Welt. Das Hafenviertel Piccola Sicilia, davon erzählen alle, war ein Ort, wo Muslime, Juden und Christen in guter Nachbarschaft lebten. Ich frage mich, ob das eine nostalgische Verklärung ist oder Wirklichkeit war. Der Benzinkanister gibt mir keine Auskunft. Als ich den Antiquitätenladen verlasse, sehe ich gegenüber die grüne Fassade der »Librairie Espace Diwan«. Ein letzter Versuch, denke ich, vielleicht reicht das Gedächtnis der Bücher tiefer als das Gedächtnis der Menschen.

Ein kleiner, feiner Laden mit kunstvollen Fotobänden, arabischer Literatur und französischen Sachbüchern. Der Buchhändler, ein diskreter und sympathischer Tunesier, zeigt mir ein Buch über die Deutschen in Nordafrika. Dann kommt der Kellner vom Café gegenüber und bringt Kaffee. Man kennt sich, man ist befreundet, und bald spricht es sich in der ganzen Gasse herum: Da ist ein Deutscher, der nach Juden sucht. Buchhändler sind wie Friseure, denke ich, die Schaltzentrale des Viertels.

»Du musst mit Jacob sprechen«, sagt der Buchhändler. »Er kann dir alles sagen, was du wissen willst.«

Alle kennen seinen Namen. Jacob Lellouche führte das letzte jüdische Restaurant der Stadt.

In La Goulette, dem Viertel am Strand, das früher, als die Italiener noch dort wohnten, auch »Piccola Sicilia« genannt wurde. Aber niemand hat seine Adresse, niemand weiß seine Telefonnummer. Das Restaurant ist geschlossen. Der Buchhändler ruft jemanden an, und zwei Gläser Kaffee später spaziert ein Mann herein, der sich als Schmuckhändler vorstellt. Drei Gläser Kaffee später verlasse ich den Buchladen zusammen mit ihm, und er führt mich zum Markt der Goldschmiede.

»Ist Jacob dort?«, frage ich.

»Nein«, sagt er. »Aber wir müssen ihm etwas mitbringen.«

Er geht in den Laden eines jüdischen Goldhändlers und kommt mit einem in ein Tuch gewickeltem Ölbild wieder heraus. Es sei nicht leicht mit den Juden, sagt er, sie seien misstrauisch, ließen nicht jeden Fremden in ihr Haus. Dieses Bild aber könnte Jacob interessieren.

Wir steigen in seinen alten Polo und fahren zum Meer, in das Viertel, das einst Piccola Sicilia hieß. Dort fragt er sich durch, bis er Jacobs Adresse erfährt. »Entrez!« Jacob Lellouche, ein mediterraner

Lebemann mit grauem Schnurrbart, Genießerbauch und philosophischem Witz, bittet uns zu Tisch.

Tatsächlich ist er misstrauisch, und ich kann ihn gut verstehen. Da kommt ein Deutscher, der über das Viertel seiner Kindheit schreibt. Was weiß der schon? Aber als ich ihm die wahre Geschichte erzähle, auf der mein Roman beruht, öffnet sich sein Herz. Er erzählt Geschichten, die in Deutschland niemand kennt: von Muslimen, die im Krieg Juden retteten.

»Auch darüber musst du schreiben«, sagt er und schildert mir, wie in seiner Kindheit Muslime, Juden und Christen ihre Feste gemeinsam feierten. »Es war keine Utopie«, sagt er. »Auch wenn damals niemand von ›Toleranz‹ sprach. Wir waren einfach Nachbarn.«

Beim Abschied packt der Schmuckhändler das mitgebrachte Bild aus. Es zeigt einen alten Rabbi, und als ich die Unterschrift des Malers sehe, stutze ich. Dort steht derselbe Name, den ich meinem Protagonisten gegeben habe: Victor Sarfati.

»Der Rabbi hat euch zusammengebracht«, lacht der Schmuckhändler. Ohne es auszusprechen, aus Respekt vor dem Rabbi, denke ich: Eigentlich war es der Buchhändler.

LIZE SPIT

Ich fand dort die Liebe.

Es passierte, als ich in der Buchhandlung nach einer passenden Karte für einen Verwandten suchte, der im Sterben lag.

Ich war mit einem Schriftstellerkollegen unterwegs, einem Mann, den ich nicht besonders gut kannte. Zusammen schauten wir die Ständer mit den Karten durch auf der Suche nach etwas, das einem Sterbenden Trost spenden könnte. Wir zeigten einander lauter Karten mit Bildern, die, im Licht des bevorstehenden Todes betrachtet, besonders sarkastisch erschienen. Es war völlig unpassend und gleichzeitig tröstlich, wir lachten nicht über den Tod des Familienmitglieds, sondern aus Erleichterung darüber, dass wir selbst weiterleben würden.

Schlussendlich wählten wir eine unverfängliche Karte mit einem Wolkenhimmel. Und ich verliebte mich in den Mann, der mit mir in der Buchhandlung vor den Ständern mit den Karten gestanden hatte. Gerade weil es so ein intimer Moment gewesen war, weil wir so schamlos und kindisch lachend da gestanden hatten, im Schatten der Trauer.

Aus dem Niederländischen von Malu Schrader

ILIJA TROJANOW

Eine Nacht im Paradies

Ein Jugendtraum: Eingesperrt zu sein unter lauten Büchern, eine ganze Nacht lang. Alleingelassen mit all der Pracht, ungestörte Zweisamkeit mit Literatur in jeglicher Form, die Ruhe, die Zeit. Paradiesisch. Im Sommer des Jahres 2017 erfüllte ich mir diesen Traum.

Nicht in einer Bibliothek, wo die Bücher schon zugerichtet sind, mit Nummern versehen wie Häftlinge, sondern in einer Buchhandlung, einer mittelgroßen, um aus dem Vollen schöpfen zu können, ohne sich zu verlaufen. Mit anderen Worten: In der Wagner'schen Buchhandlung in Innsbruck. Nach einer Nacht in dieser Wunderkammer wird einem bewusst, dass solche Buchhandlungen viel mehr als bloße Geschäfte sind. Es sind vielfältig fiebrige Kulturräume, unerlässliche Quellen für das, was wir Geist nennen und dessen Entwicklung. Solange der Mensch noch selbst denkt (manche haben diese Tätigkeit ja schon ausgelagert), wird er Buchhandlungen brauchen. Folglich benötigt jede Stadt gutsortierte intellektuelle Tankstellen.

Wer Stunden in einer Buchhandlung verbringt, gestärkt durch Wein, Aufstrich und einen disziplinlos verzehrten leckeren Kuchen, der wird getragen von einer Energie, zu finden, was dem eigenen Befinden guttun könnte. Wer oft Buchhandlungen aufsucht, wird zu einem Trüffelschwein, in der Lage, unter Tausenden von Drucksachen jene Geschichte und jene Sprache zu erschnüffeln, die das eigene Leben bereichern werden.

22.00 Uhr
Für weniger geübte, nicht traumwandlerisch zwischen den Regalen schwebenden Lesern und Leserinnen stehen am Eingang, neben der Kasse, zwei Stellwände mit »blind dates«, anonym eingepackten Büchern, die einen zu Hause überraschen sollen. Die graue Verpackung ziert eine handschriftlich verfasste Beschreibung. Die Bände seien sehr begehrt, berichtet der leitende Buchhändler, ein bärtiger Mann namens Robert Renk, ein Patriot des Buches, mit dem ich die erste Stunde verbringe, bevor er mich allein lässt. Er führt mich durch das Haus und beantwortet jede meiner Fragen, etwa »dass ein liegendes Buch sich besser verkauft als ein im Regal stehendes«.

23.00

Ich beginne bei der »Erotik«. Trotz der gesellschaftlichen Liberalisierung des Sexuellen immer noch ein wenig versteckt in einer Ausbuchtung hinten links im Erdgeschoss. Zu meinem Erstaunen erwartet mich trotz der Schwemme an kostenfreien lustverstärkenden Bildern und Filmen im Internet ein ganzer Meter Erotik. Aber wie soll ein potentieller Kunde nun das richtige Buch für sich finden? Schließlich kann er schlecht zu der netten Ute gehen und verkünden: »Ich bin 51 und stehe auf dicke Fesseln und flotte Dreier.«

Die angebotene Produktion stammt fast ausschließlich von Autorinnen, die Titel bzw. Untertitel beinhalten stets »Versuchung«, »Verlangen«, »Verführung«, »verbotene Liebe« oder »leidenschaftliches Versprechen«. Zur Erotik gehören folglich Bücher, die ohne ein »ver-« im Titel nicht auskommen können. Ich schlage auf gut Glück den Roman *Dirty Secrets* auf: »Das erste Mal war liebevoll und zärtlich und wunderschön gewesen, trotz der furchtbaren Umstände. Es war eine Flucht gewesen. Eine Befreiung.« So erotikfrei geht es weiter. Ich nippe am Weinglas und sehne mich nach Josefine Mutzenbacher.

Vielleicht kann man von einem ehemaligen Pornostar mehr erwarten. Sasha Greys Roman trägt den überraschend intellektuellen Titel *Die Janus-Kammer*. Der erste Satz bringt mich fast um den Verstand: »Menschen, die in Hotels arbeiten, vermeiden es normalerweise, in Hotels zu übernachten, und folgen damit einem weitverbreiteten Trend innerhalb der Dienstleistungsbranche.« Das ist nicht im klassischen Sinne erregend, aber immerhin informativ, wie das ganze erste Kapitel, in dem ich lerne, dass Prostituierte sich mit einem bestimmten Trick behelfen, wenn der hässliche Kerl, der auf ihnen liegt, partout nicht kommen will:

»Sie rammt ihren Mittelfinger tief in seinen Arsch hinein. Und dreht ihn im Kreis.« Aha. Leider steht aber vier Seiten weiter: »Warum nur sind harte Männerschwänze so unglaublich geschmeidig? Ist es möglich, dass die Reibung beim Masturbieren wie ein peeling wirkt?« Solche Sätze würde ich eher lesen, um den Orgasmus zu verhindern.

24.00
Die Romantik, die direkt an die Erotik anschließt, ist mit vier Metern erheblich platzeinnehmender. Die einzige Abteilung, in der ich keine der Autorin-

nen (wiederum fast nur Frauen) kenne. Auch nicht Carrie Price.

Zoe lautet ein Band aus der Reihe »New York Diaries« – Erotik und Romantik kommen meist in Reihen daher und spielen in New York, dem Liebeszentrum der Welt. Ich stolpere über den Satz: »Nach meinem niedergeschlagenen Anruf, der dieser fatalen Audition gefolgt war ...« – schlechtes Deutsch wirkt auf mich unromantisch. Der Verlag verschweigt, welche Software dieses Buch (nicht) übersetzt hat. Ich beschränke mich des Weiteren darauf, lediglich die Titel zu lesen. *Jeder Kuss ein Volltreffer*, *Ich bin zu alt für diesen Scheiß* (wie wahr!) und *Ein Cowboy küsst selten allein* (um mit offenen Karten zu spielen: Ich habe auch noch nie allein geküsst). Postmoderne Ironie allenthalben. Doch dann: *Der Junge, der mit dem Herzen sah* (es lebe der kleine Prinz) und *Das Geheimnis der Schneekirsche* – es gibt sie also noch, die pathetisch sentimentalen Titel. Ich lese in zehn beliebige Bücher hinein, alle im Stil des süßsauren Tofu-Realismus geschrieben, so austauschbar, niemand könnte sie je voneinander unterscheiden. Nach einer knappen Stunde bilde ich mir ein, die romantischen Titel riechen schlechter.

00.50

Ich wende mich etwas unbefriedigt den Verkaufs-
tischen zu, die in blauen Farben Sommerlektüre
versprechen, samt Muscheln, Korallen, Papageien,
Fischen, Sand und einer vermeintlichen Som-
merbrise. Robert Renk hatte mir das Prinzip ein-
leuchtend erklärt: »Hier ziehen die populären
Titel die weniger bekannten mit. So kann ich
einem Geheimtipp Aufmerksamkeit verschaffen.«
Donna Leon ist also die Tempoläuferin für Chris-
toph W. Bauer (es funktioniert wohl). Passend *Der
Klang der Stille* von Sergio Bambaren. Angeblich
laut Klappentext ein Buch für Mutige, also greife
ich in der Geisterstunde beherzt zu. Der erste Satz
ist eine Ohrfeige (man sollte nie ein Buch kaufen,
ohne den ersten Satz gelesen zu haben; dieser er-
zwingt zwar selten einen Kauf, spricht aber umso
häufiger eine klare Warnung aus): »Jede Minute, die
vergeht, ist eine Gelegenheit, alles zu verändern, jeder Augenblick eine Chance, alles zu verbessern.«
Wie sehr habe ich mein Leben verschwendet, was
sind all die Menschen, die ich bewundere, doch
für Luschen, da sie ein Leben lang mit gemisch-
tem Erfolg versucht haben, etwas zu verändern,
die Welt ein wenig zu verbessern. Hätten wir doch

nur Bambaren gelesen. Der paradoxe Titel wird auf Seite 34 erklärt: »Vergiss nie, dass die Stille, die du nur hörst, schwer zu finden und noch schwerer zu verstehen ist.« Ich höre im Klang der Wagner'schen Stille, wie auf einem Nebentisch Franz Schuh verächtlich schnaubt. Und Karl Kraus das Wortmesser wetzt.

Buchhandlungen sind unendlich tolerante Reiche. Hier tummeln sich Meuchelmörder der Sprache wie Herr Bambaren neben Rettern und Rittern des Wortes, wie auf dem Tisch gegenüber. Vier Bücher von des Mund-zu-Mund-Beatmers der Literatur, Alois Hotschnig, die großartige Novelle *Der Argentinier* von Klaus Merz, der Roman *Himmelfarb* meines ehemaligen Verlegers Michael Krüger, die intelligenten und gebildeten Essays von Karl-Markus Gauß. Und der so tragisch früh verstorbene David Foster Wallace, übersetzt vom Feinwerktechniker Ulrich Blumenbach, mit einer Reportage namens *Der große rote Sohn*, die zu den AVN Awards (den Oscars der Pornoindustrie) nach Las Vegas führt und sich hervorragend mit der ungewollten Parodie von Sasha Grey ergänzt. Etwas farbenübersättigt greife ich zu einem gänzlich schwarzen Band, darauf in weißen Lettern

FUTUR II. Vielversprechender geht es gar nicht, zumal das Buch vom Verbrecher Verlag stammt. Zufällig schlage ich Seite 74 auf: eine Aufzählung der Konzerte der Musikgruppe Ja, Panik über zehn Seiten hinweg. Eine neue literarische Form, der archivarische Hardcore-Numerismus. Zitat: »17.05.2010 DE. Dingolfing, Red Box Festival«. Reinster Irrsinn, nur fürchte ich, dass er ernst gemeint ist, und die Gruppe in jenem Mai tatsächlich in Dingolfing aufgetreten ist. Manchmal kommentieren sich die Publikationen: Direkt daneben liegt die neuste Ausgabe der Kulturzeitschrift Wespennest aus, zum Thema »befremden«.

01.30

Die breiten Regale mit den Krimis empfinde ich als wenig einladend, weil die Umschläge schon von weitem eine breite, uniforme rot-schwarze Front aufweisen. Offensichtlich haben die Verlage den ultimativen visuellen Köder gefunden (Schwarz für Drama, Rot für Blut), die Kunden beißen zuverlässig an, gerade weil es wenig subtil ist und daher nur noch reproduziert werden muss.

Andere Tische hingegen beschwören reihenweise persönliche Erinnerungen herauf: Michail Schischkin (ein gemeinsamer Drink in einem Zelt auf der Buchmesse), David Albahari (traurige Gespräche spät abends beim ersten Münchner Literaturfest), Michael Köhlmeier (vor kurzem eine absurde Zusammenkunft mit dem Noch-Kanzler Kern, der uns »Intellektuelle« mit einer klaren Positionierung gegen rechts übertrumpfte, die er schon am nächsten Morgen beim Kuschelgespräch mit Strache vergessen hatte), Meja Mwangi (mein erstes Tusker-Bier als Jugendlicher in Kenia, als wir aufgeregt auf einen Mwangi warteten, der nie erschien), Yu Hua (gemeinsam die Pekingente verspeist, während wir über Auflagen redeten, seine stets um eine Null höher als meine), Katja Lange-Müller (die mir neulich wie ein Rohrspatz schimpfend im Gang eines Zuges entgegenlief), T.C. Boyle (der mir erzählte, auch er höre beim Schreiben vor allem Opern, am liebsten Barockopern), Aslı Erdoğan (vor deren Gefängnis in Istanbul wir noch im November protestierten, die inzwischen freigelassen worden ist). Mir wird bewusst, wie viele Erlebnisse meines Lebens sich um Bücher und Autoren ranken, wie viele der anwesenden Kolleginnen und Kollegen ich kenne, ob persönlich oder als Leser. Es stellt sich ein rührendes Gefühl ein, als wären wir eine Familie, mit vielen Freundschaften, aber auch dem einen oder anderen schwarzen Schaf (schon fällt mein Blick auf Christian Kracht). Denn ich stehe vor der breitesten aller Regelwände, der Literatur.

02.38

Auf einmal überkommt mich ein merkwürdiger Drang aufzuräumen. Ich ordne herumliegende Exemplare ins Regal, sorge für alphabetische Ordnung, von Hector Abad bis Wu Ming. Das bereitet mir großen Spaß, danach schmerzt mir der Rücken. Es ist alles vertreten, sogar eine handsignierte Gesamtausgabe des leider noch nicht kanonisierten Edgar Hilsenrath. Natürlich mit erkennbaren idiosynkratischen Vorlieben, an denen sich die Handschrift jedes Buchhändlers zeigt: wenig von Grass, viel von Kästner; Steinfest (eine feste Burg der Phantasie) neben Stichmann (mehr Talent als Können). Viele kleine österreichische Verlage sind vertreten, das Regionale steht Schulter an Schulter neben dem Weltläufigen. Jede Menge Charmantes, Versponnenes, Bücher, die man nie von sich aus suchen würde, über die man stolpern muss, wie über Kieselsteine von ungewöhnlicher Form und Farbe.

An der »Infostelle« überrascht eine aufwendig gestaltete Monographiereihe über berühmte Autoren,
etwa über den sehr geschätzten Gottfried Benn aus
der Feder eines gewissen Jörg Magenau. Vielleicht
liegt es an der fortgeschrittenen Nachtruhe, dass
ich angesichts halbgarer Teflon-Erkenntnisse à la
»Mag sein, dass man als Pathologe eine andere Beziehung zum Tod unterhält« das Buch gleich wieder zuschlage. Mag sein, dass man als Buchhändler
eine andere Beziehung zum Lesen und als Autor
zur Sprache hat. Mag sein, wer weiß das schon so
genau …

03.44

Zeit nun für den wirklich großen Elefanten in der
Buchhandlung. Er heißt George R. R. Martin und
nimmt alleine mehr Platz ein als die Erotik und
halb so viel wie die Klassik! Tolkien hält sich wa-
cker, zu meiner Begeisterung ist Lovecraft auch
noch gut im Rennen, aber alle anderen sind mir un-
bekannt (Harry Potter ausgenommen). Erstaunlich
wie wenig man sich auskennt in gewissen Genres. Das Genre trägt übrigens den Namen Fantasy.
Science-Fiction hingegen fehlt völlig, zur ausglei-
chenden Gerechtigkeit liegt die schon legendäre

Southern-Reach-Trilogie von Jeff VanderMeer auf einem der Tische aus.

04.22

Erschöpft wende ich mich den Kalendern zu. Ich habe schon mehr Bücher in der Hand gehabt, als ich in meinem restlichen Leben werde lesen können. Diese Erkenntnis stößt mich in ein schwarzes Loch, obwohl ich zu Hause die Anwesenheit der vielen ungelesenen Bücher eher als Verheißung begreife, als Beglückung empfinde. Island und Irland scheinen besonders viele Tiroler Wände zu schmücken. Auch New York, Neuseeland und der Haderer. Welche Erkenntnisse kann man hieraus über die Einheimischen ziehen?

04.26

Ich habe das Erdgeschoß nun einmal umrundet (an den vielen Reiseführern bin ich vorbeigegangen wie ein Vegetarier an einem Metzgerladen; wer mit Reiseführern aufbricht, hindert sich selbst am Reisen). Gegenüber der Kasse – wie in jeder Buchhandlung – die Bestseller. Mal sehen, wie gut Sie sich, liebe Leser, in der Buchbranche auskennen: Die Bestseller hier stammen von Schuh, Jergović, Muschg, Bärfuss und einigen anderen. Fällt Ihnen etwas auf? Ja, wenn der Wunsch Vater des Verkaufs wäre, dann würde die Bestsellerliste in etwa so aussehen. Im real existierenden Kapitalismus aber nicht, nie und nimmer!

04.37

Hinter der Kasse in einem engen Kabuff warten die bestellten Bücher auf Abholung. Wonach gelüstet es die Innsbrucker? Nach Stanislaw Lems Meisterwerk *The Big Book of Breasts* – nein, Verzeihung, das ist der Unschärfe meines müden Blicks geschuldet, Lem steht nur unmittelbar neben einem Brustkompendium. Jemand fliegt nach Taiwan, nach Albanien oder Madagaskar, jemand will ernsthaft ins Power Training einsteigen. Jemand muss noch Mathematik lernen, jemand will alles über den Kräutergarten von Paracelsus erfahren. Es ist faszinierend: Obwohl die Wagner'sche so unendlich viel bietet, ist doch nicht für jeden alles dabei. Die Vielfalt unserer Interessen und Begierden ist eine tröstliche Vorstellung.

Auf in den ersten Stock. Hier finden sich mehr Bücher, die die Umwelt begrünen als die Welt verbessern wollen. Vielleicht weil viele glauben, mit
dem Ersteren sei es schon getan?! Es geht meter-
weit um Kochen, Esoterik und Gesundheit, aber
nur schmalregalig um Politik. Auffällig ist die Do-
minanz der individuellen Glücksversprechen. Das
Glück des Einzelnen steht öfter im Fokus als das
Glück der Gesellschaft. Obwohl Studien wiederholt
erwiesen haben, dass das Glücksempfinden der Bür-
ger in gerechteren Gesellschaften erheblich höher
ist. Anders gesagt: Soziale Ungerechtigkeit macht
die ganze Gesellschaft unglücklich. Der beste Weg,
das eigene Wohlbefinden zu steigern, wäre, das Leben aller zu verbessern. Das widerspricht aber dem
Zeitgeist, und dieser äußert sich, nicht nur in diesem Punkt, immer wieder – wie sollte es auch anders sein – in der Auswahl der Bücher. Buchhandlungen sind Seismographen der Gegenwart. Sie
können unmodische Angebote machen (viel Lyrik
und experimentelle Literatur), aber sie müssen auch
die Wünsche der Kunden respektieren. So könnte
man nach einer Nacht in der Wagner'schen den
Reichtum menschlicher Kreativität ebenso feiern

wie die dekadente Dummheit unserer Zeit beklagen.

06.06
Beim Einschlafen zähle ich anstatt Schafe Bücher,
mein Blick vom Vorübergehen der Bücherrücken so
müde, dass er nichts mehr hält.

KLAUS-PETER WOLF

Es erfüllt mich, durch Buchhandlungen zu flanieren. Ich umkreise die Tische mit Neuerscheinungen. Ich kann nicht anders. Ich muss Bücher in die Hand nehmen. Manche kaufe ich nur, weil sie sich so schön anfühlen. Bei anderen ist es ein Satz, der mich anspricht, wenn ich darin blättere.

Nicht allen Buchhändlern gefällt es, wenn jemand sich für ihre Waren so sehr interessiert, alles anfasst, unter Umständen auch wieder verwirft und zurückstellt. Aber die, die mich gewähren lassen, machen ein gutes Geschäft. Nur selten verlasse ich eine Buchhandlung mit weniger als fünf bis sechs gekauften Titeln.

Dieses Entdecken ist so toll. Die Zufälligkeit der Begegnung. Damit nicht am Ende ein Buchhändler durch seine Titelauswahl und -präsentation für mich entscheidet, besuche ich immer mehrere Buchhandlungen. Ich fühle mich dann frei und leicht. Ich gehe nicht zielgerichtet los, um ein bestimmtes Exemplar zu kaufen, ich bin offen für das, was geschieht, und ich habe Zeit. Danach sitze ich mit den gekauften Exemplaren irgendwo in der Nähe. Meist nachmittags mit einem Stück Kuchen in einem meiner Lieblingscafés.

Nein, das ist nicht von mir, sondern eine Aussage meines Serienkillers Dr. Bernhard Sommerfeldt.

Aber diese Gemeinsamkeit haben wir. Wir könnten auf vieles im Leben verzichten, aber nicht auf gute Buchhandlungen und Cafés.

ABBILDUNGSNACHWEIS

Seite 58: © Henri Matisse

Seite 62: © Andrea del Verrocchio

Seite 67: © privat

Seite 68 (oben und unten), Seite 69 (oben) und
Seite 70 (oben und unten): © Marion Brasch

Seite 69 (unten): © privat

Ich schenk dir ein Lächeln
Heitere Geschichten und Gedichte

War einmal ein Bumerang;
War ein Weniges zu lang.
Bumerang flog ein Stück,
Aber kam nicht mehr zurück.
Publikum – noch stundenlang –
Wartete auf Bumerang.

Joachim Ringelnatz

Herausgegeben von
Julia Gommel-Baharov
224 Seiten, broschiert

Weitere Informationen finden Sie auf
www.fischerverlage.de

AZ 596-90721/1